D1562010

The President of a Small College

The President of a Small College

New and Revised Edition

PETER SAMMARTINO
Chancellor, Fairleigh Dickinson University

CORNWALL BOOKS
NEW YORK • TORONTO • LONDON

Cornwall Books
4 Cornwall Drive
East Brunswick, N.J. 08816

Cornwall Books
27 Chancery Lane
London WC2A 1NF, England

Cornwall Books
Toronto M5E 1A7, Canada

Library of Congress Cataloging in Publication Data

Sammartino, Peter, 1904–
  The president of a small college.

  1. College presidents—United States. 2. Small
colleges—United States—Administration. I. Title.
LB2341.S23 1982   378'.111   82-5040
ISBN 0-8453-4757-8   AACR2

Printed in the United States of America

CONTENTS

PREFACE

I WROTE THE FIRST EDITION OF THIS BOOK ALMOST THIRTY years ago. What I felt then is basically true today. Of course, new problems have arisen: unions have taken hold in many places; women demand equal treatment, drugs have crept in, sexual mores have changed and the federal government has become inextricably involved in college matters. While the administrator of a small college has to be cognizant of all these aspects, practically everything I said in 1954 is still true today.

Are small colleges fading from the scene? I think not. After all, if we take enrollment of 2,000 as a cut-off figure, about two thirds of the public and private colleges in the United States are small colleges. In addition, many of the undergraduate colleges of large universities are really small colleges. Moreover, I believe fervently that small colleges may be the real answer to problems of higher education. Let me cite a story to illustrate what I mean. When I wrote the original book, Fairleigh Dickinson College was a very small institution. As we got larger, I found we were losing some of the virtues of a small institution. For that reason, I established Edward Williams College, a two-year institution limited to 400 students. Through the generosity of Senator Fairleigh S. Dickinson, I was able to have a special building in Hackensack, New Jersey, for the new unit. What I proposed to do was to break up the first two years of our university into small colleges of about 400 each to be followed by a three year segment leading directly to the master's degree. Another friend, Leonard Dreyfuss, enabled me to establish a pilot college, Leonard Dreyfuss College, on our Madison Campus. I know from my experiment that we can do much more for students in small colleges and, as a matter of fact, we found that the graduates of Edward Williams College did much better when they transferred into the junior year than the regular university students, whether it was at our own institution or in other universities.

One may ask, won't small colleges drop from the scene as the private secondary schools did? I don't think so, for two reasons. First, the old-time academies had relatively small investments; those that had extensive campuses survived. Second, when public high schools appeared it made sense to keep younger people at home and attending the high school in the community. But note that as public high schools became too large, and were beset by problems, there was a renaissance of the private school, both nonsectarian and religious. I believe the same thing will take place as far as small private colleges are concerned, although I concede that every year some will close their doors because of indifferent promotion and poor administration. I firmly believe that the small college, operated on a sound financial basis, led by an imaginative administrator and with an enlightened and progressive faculty, will be able to offer an education that is superior to that of a large institution where the student is lost in the crowd, whose faculty becomes a group of lost souls adding a bit here and there in assembly line procedures.

The chances for survival of the small college are better than ever. There is an opportunity for more effective service to the students and there is the advantage of avoiding the confusion, the duplication, the anonymity of the massive institutions.

This little book is meant for the administrator or the prospective administrator of a small college. It is not meant for the president of a large institution whose administrative organization would naturally be different. I must also add that since there is a wide dissimilarity among even the small colleges, it is almost impossible to suggest patterns that may fit all institutions. I believe that this is true: a college evolves its administrative pattern around the persons it has on its staff. It should be the other way around: the staff should be selected to fit a preconceived system. But actually what does happen isn't too bad because it means utilizing the strength of the persons already employed.

I should like to make this one point very strongly. I do not claim that mechanical details are the most important things in a college. Quite the contrary. What I do say is that it is wise to take care of the non-educational problems of a college and get them out of the way so that the major attention can be focused on instruction and guidance. And whether he or she likes it or not, whether he or she thinks it fair or unfair, the president of a small college must fill many more roles than the one he or she would choose: that of a real educator in the broadest and finest sense of the word.

Naturally, I hope that other administrators, especially the neophytes, may derive some little value from this book. I think that it might be a good thing for presidents of other small colleges to write about their experiences and ideas. I found the greatest enjoyment in listening to other administrators talk about their solutions to problems. There were always points which were helpful to me and would reinforce or expand my way of thinking.

There are many fine books on college administration but they are concerned primarily with large institutions or with broad philosophic matters. I emphasize that the educational goals of an institution are of primary importance. But I have seen institutions with worthwhile objectives disintegrate because of poor administration and I have seen institutions with nebulous educational philosophy take root because people came along to put them in administrative order and then were able to superimpose a philosophic entity. I make this final statement. An administrator can accomplish nothing unless the faculty and other members of his staff work along with him. If all work together, these problems become virtually nonexistent.

I am extremely appreciative of the college presidents who read the manuscript and offered suggestions:

Dr. Rose M Channing, President, Middlesex
    Community College,
Dr. Donald Grunewald, President, Mercy College,
Dr. Delmont N. Merrill, President, Husson College,
Admiral E. A. Rogers, Superintendent, Maine
    Maritime Academy,
Dr. Louis V. Wilcox, Jr., President, Unity College.

I am grateful for the patient help of my secretary, Mrs. Mavis Hemsley.

Peter Sammartino

Rutherford, New Jersey
November 12, 1981

1

THE PRESIDENT'S LIFE

BEING PRESIDENT OF A COLLEGE IS AN AWESOME RESPONSI-
bility. It means being the leader, the catalyst, the administrator, the father-confessor, the slave of an
academic community. It means the responsibility for
making sure that the students receive the best education, the best educational guidance, the most rational
physical and nutritional direction possible, and enjoy
the most helpful social climate. It means leading the
faculty to the highest professional level. It means the
responsibility for integrating the services of the non-
teaching staffs and providing a suitable quality of life for
them. It means making sure that the college blends with
the community in which it is located.

Life is living out ideals. The presidency of a college
means an opportunity to achieve ideals that are rarely
within the grasp of business, industrial or other professional fields. The president has to work hard and relatively long hours so that he or she may not be accused
of not solving problems because he or she was too lazy

to work a few more hours that day or that week. The president must have the willingness and capacity to study questions, absorb details, listen patiently to conflicting views and then make decisions as justly as possible. He has to have humility and compassion as he deals with the inevitable human dilemmas that face him. And he has to have the common sense, the balance, to keep in physical and nutritional shape and not allow himself to retogress healthwise.

It won't be easy and, often the question is: "Is it worth it?" The answer is "yes." Someone has to be a leader; the élan of life is in leading. As one leads, one creates, whether it is a family, or an industrial operation, or a political entity. But shepherding a college has a special cachet of its own even though it may not have the financial concomitant or the publicity of other life responsibilities.

The college president's job is a difficult one for two reasons. First, he is under constant pressure from the community, from the faculty, from the students, and perhaps from the trustees. Second, if he is conscientious about his job, he will be thinking of his work twenty four hours a day. All the more reason why he should be careful about his personal life so that it may counterbalance the vigorous professional requirements that face him.

First he should have a comfortable and well appointed office. He is going to spend more hours in his office than in his own living room. It should be cheerful and relaxing. Aside from the fact that it is good public relations for the college, an inviting office means less wear on the chief officer. I make this point because many college presidents—perhaps to set an example of frugality—carry on in offices that would insult a shipping clerk. A seedy looking office is false economy for the college and for the president.

Second, the college president must decide how much leisure time he wants to have. True, there will always be something to interfere with his plans, but if he doesn't make a tentative schedule, he will be working night and day seven days a week. One college president told me he figured out that on the basis of the number of hours he put in, he was the lowest paid member of the staff. I propose that a president limit himself to a fifty-five hour week. It sounds silly, doesn't it? And yet, if he is conscientious, he will rarely be able to put in fewer hours, and there is a danger that he may burn himself out by putting in many more hours. I schedule the fifty five hours as follows: a nine-hour day, five days a week; three hours allotted to two evenings a week for special meetings; four hours during the week end. The remainder of the time he should try to forget the college.

I believe the matter of food is important in the life of a college president. First, he is apt to have his meals at irregular hours. He may find himself eating so many restaurant or hotel meals that he will soon have a stomach ailment or put on excess fat. I recommend that the president limit outside luncheons or dinners to two a week, and, even then, to be abstemious unless he has a cast iron stomach.

A word about drinking is in order. Some years ago, I was going to a convention with another college president. We went to the dining car, and sat down, and soon the hovering steward was asking whether we wanted a cocktail. My colleague looked around nervously and explained that he wanted to make sure that no trustee happened to be around. That seemed to me to be ridiculous. I know some of his trustees. They all enjoy a drink now and then. Why should they limit the personal freedom of their chief executive? A member of a college faculty ought to feel free to act as any other member of society. If he feels like having a cocktail before dinner, he should have it, and, if he doesn't like to drink, he should not be expected to have it just to prove he is a regular fellow.

Regarding vacations, a president ought to have a generous vacation. He'll do a lot of creative thinking anyway about the college while he is away from it. It will be relaxed thinking and it will produce dividends for the institution. Naturally, there should be a responsible person on hand at the college at all times.

I believe it is absolutely essential for a college president to have outside interests and friends divorced from the institution. There is so much danger that he may get into a rut. Life can become simply the ending of one college meeting and the beginning of another. The importance of his position demands that he keep up an active interest in cultural phases of living, the theatre, music, literature, the arts. And while it certainly is to be recommended that he try to continue an active role in what was his own special field before he became an administrator, it also behooves him to be above average in his understanding and appreciation of the finer things of life. I emphasize this point because too many presidents make themselves martyrs to their work and cease living culturally. In the end they do a disservice to their profession. A college president should be a cultural leader, not a stick-in-the-mud. He should set the example for his faculty and not encourage them to follow him in cultural backsliding.

He will need to have friends from outside the college circle and by that I don't mean those he meets at the weekly meeting of a service club. He needs friends from other fields and he needs conversation that will not concern itself with higher education. Most of this social activity should be with his wife and children as active participants. There is always a grave danger that in trying to keep up with the duties of his job, the college executive may neglect his family. No job is important enough, no institution should be selfish enough to require its chief executive to sacrifice his home life. Finally, a college executive has the right to privacy. If he doesn't insist upon it to some extent, he will soon find that students, parents, community representatives, and even faculty will be calling at his door or on the phone at all hours and on all days including Sundays. This does not preclude the fact that he must be available at all times for real emergencies.

There is one last word—a college president needs above all a sense of humor. He needs to realize that the college can go on without him, that people will be thoughtless at times, that matters which loom large at the moment will be unimportant tomorrow, and that other people are as imperfect as he is. In other words, he has to learn to take things in his stride and to find in each day a few hours to enjoy life outside of his career.

In the following chapters, I shall discuss many things that have to be done by the college president, but are never thought of as part of the administrative functions. The head of a college has to be a man of creative ability, a person who thinks in terms of broad educational philosophy, a man or woman who can build up the value of the college to the community and to the students it serves. The president of a small college must also be an able business administrator, a person who can maintain an *esprit de corps* among his custodial, clerical, and teaching staffs, an individual who can watch details before they become major dilemmas. If he or she has the business ability without the broad philosophic qualities, he or she is not a true college president. But if he has only the latter qualities, there is grave danger that the institution will flounder on economic rocks unless he is blessed with extremely able assistants or enjoys the income from a fabulous endowment fund.

2

THE COLLEGE BEEHIVE

IT IS MY BELIEF THAT THE MAJORITY OF COLLEGE PRESIDENTS work too hard. They are under constant pressure because if anything goes wrong they are probably going to bear the blame no matter whose fault it is. Conversely, they also share the glory when there is a merited pat on the back. Especially in a small institution, everything eventually drops into the president's lap. All he has to do is to walk around the campus and he can pick up half a dozen problems. Or let him stand in a main hallway for a few minutes and the problems will run up to him. Just when he thinks he has taken care of everything for a few days and his desk is cleared, in comes a batch of work. Veritably, like the Queen in *Alice in Wonderland,* "it takes all the running you can do to keep in the same place."

Sometimes a president focuses his attention on his next job. The present one is simply a stepping stone. This isn't bad if he works conscientiously on the current one. But if he or she spends his time on projects just to get publicity and engages in a variety of professional activities to the neglect of the job he or she is being paid for, then the president is not being fair to the profession. In some cases, the public relations director concentrates on building up the president practically to the exclusion of everything else. He may soon forget that college is a cooperative affair, that the college comes first, and that the president is decidedly in a secondary category.

Then there are those new presidents who would like to enter into the blood stream of a college but are prevented from doing so because of vested interests within the institution which guard jealously the status quo and resent any changes. No boy scout is going to show them what to do! If there has been only one faculty meeting a semester before he came, woe be unto him if he decides to have two a semester. If Professor Smith has gotten into the habit of having all his classes on Tuesday, Wednesday, and Thursday, so that he can have long weekends, the only way he can be made to change without a fight is to double his salary.

During a boom period, adjustments are easier to make. There is enough money to go around and money can help solve a lot of problems and soothe a lot of ruffled feelings. The trouble comes during periods of retrenchment. Then the eruptions occur. Departmental vested interests put on extra guards. There is a general lowering of morale, and prexy had better pull a rabbit out of the hat or else!

But great emergencies may produce great changes. I shall never forget a meeting of college presidents held in Baltimore in January of 1942, following Pearl Harbor. High government officials discussed with us how to organize for war. Then we broke up into smaller groups so that each one could describe how he would meet the new challenge. One man said, "This will give me a wonderful opportunity to make some of the changes I've wanted to make for years." What he was admitting was that he had been powerless to do the things he felt should be done at his college.

All of this wrestling and tugging is unfortunate, and there is a way of overcoming it. The faculty should have a fairly good concept of the general administrative and financial problems facing an institution. Too many college professors feel that they are kept out of the general sphere of the big brass. On the other hand, too many burrow a little hole for themselves and don't want to know anything except their own specialty. Both are wrong points of view. Every member of the faculty should know how he fits into the general scheme of things. Fortunately for the small college, this is relatively easy to accomplish. Every faculty member ought to participate in as many ways as possible in the thinking and in the working of administration.

A step in this direction is the monthly meeting of the whole faculty which functions somewhat as a seminar on in-service training or growth. These meetings should not be formal meetings in the parliamentary sense. They should be free discussions where people can learn from one another, where they can grow and learn to create. Some of the topics for discussion might be: new curricula, revisions of existing ones, library, general college promotion, plans for new buildings, guidance, social activities, administrative procedures, alumni organization, objectives of the college, admission of students, catalogue, faculty welfare, and any other general matters affecting the progress of the institution.

From time to time, perhaps it might be well to have one's own or an outside expert lead the discussion. For instance, it might be helpful to have a reading expert lead a series of discussions on reading so that instructors of various subjects can strengthen student reading habits. Colleges today are apt to get students with wide variations in reading ability. Professors, in general, do not have the expertise to guide students' reading. A college education is basically a reading education. Discussion, laboratory and clinical work, out-of-class experiences, all these have to be coordinated with reading. Once a year it makes sense to have a discussion on reading. Students with poor reading habits may have to take a reading course. In my school of dentistry, even though we had a very selective group (one acceptance out of 22 applications and all with bachelors' degrees) I insisted on having the students take a reading course. Why? Because the faster they read, the better they could master their professional material and the more chances there were that they would carry on their professional reading after graduation.

Professors have to be taught how to guide their students in effective reading. The college library has to coordinate with the faculty because today, with moderate-cost paperbacks, it is well to encourage students to build their lifetime libraries, to mark up their paperbacks and to make their study effective. All of this does not happen by itself. Many faculty members need as much guidance as the students.

Another area of discussion is that of applying for grants: what federal and state agencies to apply to, how to get foundation addresses, examples of effective applications. I would encourage adequate secretarial help when necessary. Discussions are bound to produce some results. Allied to this topic is that of getting contributions and here the discussion leader should be the director of development.

Now these general faculty seminars should not interfere with regular departmental meetings, with standard faculty committees or with special committees. Inciden-tally, I have found that young members of the faculty are needlessly in awe of the administrative officers and of older persons on the staff. For this reason I had a very informal and unofficial committee of five young people whose business it was to make suggestions for the bet-ter utilization of younger persons on the faculty. They proposed membership on certain committees and were free to discuss any matter affecting their welfare.

I believe we can realize how fortunate a small institu-tion is if we discuss the defects of large institutions. The larger the institution, the more impersonal it becomes. Communication becomes difficult both among faculty and students. As a result, the persons at the top do not have a clear understanding of how policies affect faculty or students.

Another great disadvantage of large size is that it takes more time to get things done. In one institution a matter has to go to the committee on agenda, which then decides when it may come up before the general faculty, which in turn delegates it to a special commit-tee, which then reports back to the general faculty. In many cases, by the time a decision is reached, the need is no longer there. The same holds true with other im-portant phases of instruction, such as the library acces-sions. The individual instructor submits requests to the head of department, who in turn submits all the re-quests to the dean or perhaps to a library committee or both. The librarian finally gets the list and, by the time the books come in, the course or the instructor may have disappeared. It is obvious that the small institution can avoid circuitous routes and preserve the valuable elements of personal understanding and of quick deci-sions. But too often small institutions give up these valuable assets in order to copy the systems in vogue in larger institutions.

3

DEPARTMENTAL ORGANIZATION

WHAT SHOULD THE DEPARTMENTAL HIERARCHY BE IN A small college? There are many who feel there should be a clear cut line of authority somewhat in a military fashion. Where the pattern is established through a strict civil service procedure, it is indeed a straight jacket that can not be avoided. But a great many handicaps of the system are often overlooked. Too often we like to have lines of authority drawn neatly on a page as if we were working out a military system or playing with toy soldiers. And why should anyone take it for granted that a military system is the best?

What are some of the wrong assumptions we make? First, in a college of two thousand or less, department faculties are not all the same size. The English department may have twenty five or thirty, some other may have just one or two persons. And the minute you emphasize departments, the one with one or two immediately thinks in terms of becoming larger. Whether it makes sense or not, or whether there exist college or

community needs, are all matters of secondary importance. The main point is that, for professional prestige,
the larger the department the better. The ugly head of
departmental vested interests begins to leer at us.

Second, the creation of departments is at best one
that varies according to the subjective ideas of the head
of the institution or according to the influence of faculty
members who want to become heads of departments.
In one college, speech, journalism, literature, creative
writing, dramatics may all be separate departments. In
another, they may be all together in one department.
Obviously, departments do not have a standard professional delineation. Sometimes a teacher is a really
strong promoter and probably with some justification
brings forth the importance of his or her work.

Third, the method of becoming a department varies
from college to college, and varies within the college.
What are some of the reasons that lead to the designa-
tion of a department chairman?

1. Today, the current fashion seems to have the
    chairman elected by members of the depart-
    ment. This has advantages and disadvantages.
    It tends to give the chairman the coloration of a
    shop steward and while this may jibe with un-
    ion techniques—if there is a union—it does not
    always make for strong professional leadership.
    It also leads to political maneuvering and to quid
    pro quo. In one case in a department of three
    persons, for instance, there were two candi-
    dates, each one of whom voted for himself. The
    third person really decided who the chairman
    was to be, a power he did not fail to draw upon
    when recommendations for promotion were
    made. In a small college there has to be a judi-
    cious balance between the wishes of the depart-

ment and good administrative direction. A good chairman is not simply a clerk-of-the-works, nor is he the representative of the faculty in demands on the trustees and the administration. However, this does not mean that being near to his faculty members, he can not pass along to the president their feelings and their reactions.

2. He may be the senior in age or experience.
3. He may have created his own department.
4. He may have been on the ground floor as it grew up.
5. He may have been called in to strengthen and build up his department.
6. He may be a scholar of outstanding merit, and it may be to the institution's credit to have him listed as a department head.
7. His subject could not be classified with any other department so that it was left swimming by itself.
8. The particular person could not get along with the department chairman he really should be with so, for the sake of harmony, he was left alone.
9. The institution may want to highlight for public relations purposes a particular subject that a department head is created to give it prestige. Sometimes, and this may be because of State regulation the department may even be called a School!

Fourth, different chairmen have different strengths and different weaknesses. Therefore, to expect the same degree of cooperation from each in each different area is unrealistic. No, the army setup doesn't function at all perfectly in a small college.

But, suppose one did have a perfect organization and one could depend on perfect coordination. What might be expected of a department chairman?

1. He can seek his own new instructors and recommend their appointment.
2. He can observe his instructors and suggest ways of improvement.
3. He can develop course syllabi in cooperation with his department members.
4. He can foster experiments and research within his department.
5. He can be responsible for any administrative reports required of his instructors.
6. He can initiate and assume responsibility for public relation projects affecting his department. This means he must be a fairly good speaker and have a sense of promotional publicity.
7. He can be the leader and father-confessor of the members of his departmental group and make sure they are all happy in their work.
8. He can assume direction for the guidance of students whose major progress within the college depends on the courses within his department.

Now if it is clearly understood that these shall be the chief functions of the department head, the president will really have strong aids in the administration of the college. If colleges can get such heads of departments, and in addition be sure that these heads will always act in the best interests of the college first, they will have achieved administrative perfection. In other words, the ideal department head must do all of the things enumerated and yet keep his department in balance with the true purpose of the college.

Now what are the shortcomings, dangers or bad habits that a department chairman can have?

1. He may not be adept in finding new instructors. Perhaps he will do what is too often done in education, take the first one who comes along.

Or perhaps he may staff his department with friends. This need not be a fault, because most often we know more about friends than about total strangers.

2. He may become soft-hearted and not weed out weak faculty members.
3. He may want to build up his department beyond reasonable limits simply for the prestige.
4. He may fail to build a progressive spirit of research and experimentation.
5. He may neglect to encourage his faculty in strong and effective teaching, in the accomplishment of results and in good guidance.
6. He may be a milquetoast in public relations or he may go to the other extreme and be a publicity hog with embarrassing repercussions for the college.
7. He may be irrational in the treatment of his faculty and induce a low morale in his department.

The personal popularity of the head of the department is something else again. It may have nothing to do with the real worth of the chairperson. Faculty members will prefer on one hand to be left alone and have as little visible administration as possible. They will prefer this until they get to the point where they feel their real worth is not being adequately recognized. Then they will wish that the head of the department were more active administratively and know what is going on.

The important thing is for the head of the department to be pleasantly active and to do some administration every day. If he lets it pile up and tries to do it all in a few days, it becomes meaningless and ineffective. Common sense would dictate that he be just and objective in the assignment of classes and programs. He has to be benevolent and kindly, and yet he has to be firm in expecting his men and women to adhere to the standards of the college and of the department. And above all, he must realize that everything he does is to help the individual students and that departmental organization is merely a device to effect better service for them.

4

PUBLIC RELATIONS

PUBLIC RELATIONS HAS BECOME ONE OF THE FANCIEST TERMS in our vocabulary. In its essence, the term simply means common sense applied to the relations of the college with student body, alumni, parents, high schools, and community.

A good administrator will work for good relations as a matter of course. The trouble, however, is that he won't always be able to get press notices on what he is accomplishing. What he needs, therefore, is a good publicity person. Public relations people have banished this awful term from the vocabulary of their trade.

Now it is true that some college presidents spend too much time on one phase or another, whether it be fundraising or feeding the students or curriculum development. As a result they may need help in neglected areas, whether they be alumni organization or promotion among the high schools or student activities. In that case an alumni secretary or a field representative or a director of activities may be needed.

The problem of keeping the public informed is important. Again, let us consider the problem from the point of view of the small college. The larger colleges and universities can afford to have large staffs covering all the angles. In many cases, the person in charge of a university public relations office becomes an executive of the institution. And of course, he will have assistants—photographers, secretaries and stenographers.

The small institution is lucky if it can have one publicity person. That person has to find and screen his or her own news, and, in most cases, type it, make stencils and send out the releases. In many cases, and I strongly recommend it, he or she will have one or more student helpers. The mechanics of such an office are important because, in most cases, the staff is working against time, especially if the college is situated in an area where there are morning and afternoon papers to be serviced. Inevitably, there will also be some weeklies, and then the problem arises of preventing one paper from "scooping" another.

It is good practice to have one important story released for the weekly paper deadline so that the weekly can have fresh news in each issue. Other events have to be publicized on the spot and then, of course, the weekly has to decide whether it wants to reprint news already covered in the dailies. Sometimes, this problem can be solved by giving the weekly some special home town angle that gives an old story a new twist.

If you are a very small institution, you may be able to afford only one paid person. Make sure this person realizes that he or she is not the head of an empire but must do the typing, xeroxing, folding, sealing and mailing involved. The job has to be finished from beginning to end and integrated into the newspaper deadlines.

Often the college may not be able to afford a seasoned

public relations person and may have to train its person. All the more reason why the president of a small college has to know something of college publicity.

Most often, the president will have to train a person who has had no experience in publicity work. Is it an impossible task? Not necessarily. It simply requires common sense and intelligent planning. As a matter of fact, I have always felt I preferred a person who had a good college background and just ordinary common sense to a professional without these attributes. The training period should not take over one week, and should include:

1. Reading two or three books on college public relations.
2. Looking over the college's clipping book.
3. Reading the college catalogue and other informative material.
4. Knowing the college plant.
5. Knowing the main newspapers to be serviced and their deadlines. A visit to the main newspaper offices to introduce himself or herself might be in order.
6. Knowledge of the mechanics of the office.
7. A quick briefing on outstanding personages at the college, familiarity with current experiments and research, faculty highlights, troublesome problems, things the college is famous for, and perhaps main events of the year.

If the person has a desire to succeed and has a flair for publicity, he or she will take on from there.

Now, of course, publicity work can be divided roughly into two classes: the news release for some event at the college, and the special story on some phase of the college's activity. The first is relatively easy because the newspapers will want it and, in many cases, will send their own reporters to get the story. The second takes imagination and resourcesfulness. It is not the purpose of this chapter to repeat what is so well told in some of the good books on college publicity. But I do recommend that the publicity person be given some incentive to write special stories. Usually these stories have to be thought out after office hours, and some kind of bonus system may be an equitable way of compensating for the creative endeavor.

The matter of photography is another problem. A small institution can not afford a full-time photographer. Usually, however, some arrangement can be made with a local photographer to give quick service to the college. In order to expedite matters, it might help matters to have a small laboratory for the photographer to use. The ideal is for the college messenger to be on the way to the newspapers with a press photo within an hour after the event.

A word about students. I approve highly of using student assistants both for publicity releases and for other tasks. Of course, they must be supervised and directions must be clear cut. I have found that they always rise to the challenge and do good work. It is good for students to have a part in the publicity policies of the college. Like everything else, students need leadership and they need frank criticism. Generally, we seem to oscillate between two extremes: either no student participation or a completely free hand. I believe that when it comes to publicity, it is well from time to time to explain to the entire student body the need for public information and for accurate releases, and then to call from the group those students who want to work on public relations.

However, I emphatically do not wish to imply that

public relations are not important. I believe that every administrator, every teacher has to be cognizant of its importance. I believe further that as a college increases in size, it has to have one officer whose main attention will be on public relations. It seems to me that schools of education would do well to develop such persons, from the field of education. I do not believe we want the glib Hollywood public relations person in education. We do want, however, persons who know education, have had experience in it, and know how to work out the mechanics of good communication with the public.

Now let us take up some negative aspects and some things to watch out for. This is not a position for a disorganized person. Nor is it a sinecure for someone who wants two or three hours a day. The president should look over the clippings once a week and comment upon them to the publicity person. Files of releases, of photographs, of clippings have to be kept neatly not only for the present but for archival purposes.

Look out for the person who talks a good line but does not produce. The test is: how many articles were printed? How many special features? How many photographs? The president should be able to distinguish between special articles that have originated with the publicity person and those that have originated with the newspaper.

From time to time, unfortunate events are bound to take place. Rape, murder, malfeasance, student rebellions, strikes by students or faculty or other employees, fires, drunken brawls, drugs, you name them. If you are president long enough, most, if not all of them, will happen. Make up a list of what calamities could happen and decide that when the worst takes place, you will maintain your composure. You'll take things in your stride. You may be fortunate enough to have a dean or some other administrator who will quench the fire or placate the students or the parents for you. There are some things you must do. One, is to have the facts even if you stay in the background. Two, to support the person who is handling the problem. If he is helpless and simply founders and throws the problem into your lap, then he may not be the person you want. I have always found it advisable to have a short statement written out in case the newspaper or television station requires one. I have insisted that the entire statement be used and for that reason, brevity is important. Most times, I have never used the statement. Having such a statement ready avoids the possibility of being rushed into inane or faltering remarks. You need to remain calm, be available if necessary, and think ahead. If the problem is a fire, for instance, it might be well to think immediately of how the lack of the facilities burning will be made up, how the financial problem, temporary or permanent, will be solved. Trustees are bound to ask questions. Have answers ready for them. And make sure you have the facts straight. You may have to call up parents and go through the ordeal of telling them the bad news. If the happening is important enough, you may have to report on it at the next trustees' meeting or you may have to issue a special statement to them by mail. You may find it expedient to state what measures you are taking to avoid the catastrophe in the future; this after discussing the matter with administrative assistants and the faculty. In some cases, discussion with students, with secretaries or with custodial staff may produce important suggestions.

If it is a strike, you may be forced to issue a series of newspaper statements. Make sure each statement is brief so that it can be printed in full. Read over each sentence and see how it sounds by itself in case it is lifted out of context.

When you have done everything you can and organized for the future, relax and go on to your next job.

5

EVALUATION OF INSTRUCTORS

HOW ARE INSTRUCTORS TO BE EVALUATED? IS IT BY SOME arcane process, by gossip, by fleeting personal impressions? Is it simply by the amount of published material? I believe that the fairest way is to have student evaluation. If everyone is subject to the same process of evaluation, it becomes an acceptable democratic procedure. The form I devised was simple and it took no more than five minutes a semester (see top of next page).

The sheet should be filled out in at least two of the instructor's classes, chosen at random in most cases. Sometimes, it might be well to choose a class where there has been some maladjustment or in a new course. It has been my experience that students are extremely fair. Once in a while a disgruntled student tries to get back at an instructor, but he or she can be quickly spotted. In a very small college, the president should read all of these returns; after all the evaluation of his faculty is probably his most important job. The dean and the chairman should certainly read them. The instructors should have the right to look at the sheets.

Student's Rating of Instructor

This is an unusual responsibility! Be fair and accurate!

Name of Instructor.................... Subject.............. Date.......

	Above Average	Average	Below Average
Command of subject matter			
Enthusiastic attitude toward subject			
Ability to explain clearly			
Sympathetic attitude toward students			
Effective personality			

State any exceptional qualities of the instructor
or any difficulties you may be having

Is such a procedure perfect? Of course not. But it does make instructors aware of their weaknesses and it does point out a number of matters which can be easily remedied. For instance, sometimes textbooks are either too difficult or are not being used. Or perhaps the instructor doesn't speak loudly enough, or perhaps the students feel the need of more laboratory work, or any number of things.

The sheets can be scored: three points for "above average," two points for "average," one point for "below average." Fifteen is a perfect score. I found that anything below eleven indicated trouble.

There are many rating sheets I have seen that are more complete and seek to measure many more things. I think it is important to use a device that can be read and interpreted quickly.

FROM: Hamden L. Forkner

TO: Students in the Department of Business
           and Vocational Education

I am eager to get your reactions to various experiences you have had
at Teachers College this session. Will you please help me by taking a
few minutes to fill out the form below.

List below by course name the courses you have taken this session	Assuming you had a friend who had the same objectives you have, please indicate below what advice you would give him		
	You would recommend the course	You would recommend it with reservations because	You would not recommend it because

If the following courses had been available to you this session indicate
which courses you would have liked to take by placing a check mark
in front of the name of the course.

> Preparation and use of visual materials in business education.
> Community resources and their use in business education.
> This would be largely a field trip course to business and industrial
> firms.
> Work experience in business education in which you would work
> in a business office full-time and meet in a seminar two or three
> evenings a week for four to six points of credit. You would, of
> course, be paid on a regular basis.

Are there any other courses that you would have liked to have had
available in the department?
What kind of information or help should Teachers College or the department have provided you before you came here to study?
What are some of the things that irritated you during the session that
better planning would have avoided?
What are some of the things that you particularly enjoyed at Teachers
College or in the department that you think we should continue or do
more of to make your session more profitable and pleasant?

COMMENTS:

The blank we used is far from perfect, but it has the advantage of being brief. Professor Hamden L. Forkner, Jr., of Teachers College, Columbia University, approached the problem from another angle. His questionnaire was intended to evaluate a course, and probably that is equally important as the evaluation of the teacher, although there is a vast area of overlapping.

If we are going to evaluate instructors, then it becomes equally necessary to evaluate administration. It might be a very good thing to have such a blank filled out by instructors every few years. This is the form I used at Fairleigh Dickinson College while we were small and I was president.

Faculty Questionnaire on Administration

(Faculty members are requested to return questionnaire unsigned, in a sealed envelope, and also to explain answers, especially negative ones.)

1. Do you feel that the Administration encourages experimentation and freedom in using new techniques?
2. Are there opportunities for socializing experiences among the faculty?
3. Do you feel that there is present in the College a "climate for adjustment?"
4. Do you feel a sense of belonging?
5. Do you feel a sense of security at Fairleigh Dickinson?
6. Do you feel at all hesitant to talk over any grievances with the president?
7. Do you feel he really listens to your suggestions or grievances?
8. Do you feel a sense of frustration in anything?
9. Do you feel recognition is given for a job well done?
10. Do you feel that you have a part in the development of the College?
11. Do you feel that you have freedom to criticize?
12. Realizing physical and financial limitations, are there any specific recommendations you should like to make?

This form is filled out anonymously and I have personally profited a great deal from it. When the returns came in, I used to discuss some of the points brought up in the blanks. An administrator should have a sort of humorous humility as he discusses his shortcomings. Theoretically, any instructor ought to feel free to speak to the president on any of the matters, but, of course, there is a natural shyness on the part of many to do so.

How else can we evaluate members of the faculty? Classroom observation is another means, and a very important one. There should be frequent observation of new instructors and less frequent ones of older members of the faculty as a regular part of the administrative procedures within the college. These observations should be made by at least three different persons, probably the head of department, the dean, and the president. At least, these visits will give you an idea of the best the instructor is capable of.

When I established the Madison campus of our university, I wanted to make sure that I had a good cadre of teachers to start with and set the standards. I took some instructors from our other two campuses and appointed new ones. And then after two months, I asked three college presidents, as consultants, each to observe each one of the twenty or so members of the faculty and to give me a frank and objective report. I am glad to say, each one went through with flying colors. But more important, it was an exhilarating experience for the faculty to know how well they had done. It was, of course, of great value to me to have the three presidents tell me that we had organized the new campus with a good founding faculty.

What else can be measured? The professional activity of the instructor is important, although this may often be misleading and may indeed be a cover-all for serious defects. But it is important as one aspect of the person's entire pattern. The usefulness to the college in general guidance and administrative matters is to my mind more important. I believe for instance that every instructor ought to know the catalogue quite thoroughly. If every instructor can be a sort of first-aider in guidance, the college is immeasurably stronger. Ninety per cent of the guidance problems are routine and can be answered easily by any person familiar with the catalogue. But how many times have you seen a student waiting endlessly to see some harassed administrative officer, when any instructor should have been able to give him the answer.

Details of administrative procedures are not the most important things in the college, but they are a necessary part of the institution's existence. There are a few times during the year when special duties have to be done, such as registrations, social activities, commencement plans, and recording. Everybody has to pitch in and prima donnas are definitely unneeded. Everything else being equal, the faculty member who cooperates in the necessary chores of administration and who participates actively in being a source of guidance to students is much the stronger one.

A small college can not afford to have uncooperative persons. I have found that the greatest minds, the best ones of the faculty, are the most cooperative. I think it is important that the president himself be ever ready to pitch in and lead the faculty in some humble task. But occasionally you have a bumbling person who somehow is a good instructor, who is basically conscientious but who is all thumbs when it comes to cooperating on some mechanical task. How do you handle him? The best thing is not to let him get in your way.

Who finally decides that an instructor is not to stay? Let us not be concerned with the instructor who is patently impossible and after the first year the decision is a very obvious one. Let us discuss the person who is on the borderline, but who is not a good risk for tenure.

In a small college, it is probably best to have a carefully chosen committee of ten persons, all of whom already have tenure and have reached the highest rank, and have them make the recommendations. It is my belief that a faculty member will rise to the full challenge of this task which, after all, is probably the most important in the college. Such a committee will have to concern itself with the work of a new instructor right up to the point of achievement of tenure. Recommendations to the committee can be made by the president, by the dean, by the departmental chairman, or by any of its members. Discussions should be quite frank but objective. The committee submits its recommendations to the president and then to the Board of Trustees which has the final legal authority.

The obvious advantage of such arrangement is that ten persons will probably be less subjective than any one administrator. Of course, such a plan will need fifteen or twenty years of experience to be evaluated properly. I believe the plan will succeed for two reasons. First, the men and women on this committee are imbued with a high sense of professional responsibility. Second, it would be to their disadvantage to freeze into the college persons of weak ability.

Two other types of evaluative blanks are given here. The first is really an observation report made up by a dean.

Observation Report

Instructor Observed

Subject   Date

Not Evident / Inadequate / Fair / Good / Excellent

1. The Instructor (Teaching Personality)
   a. Presence before the class

Excellent
Good
Fair
Inadequate
Not Evident

  b. Voice, speech and use of English
  c. Vitality and enthusiasm
  d. Command of subject matter
  e. Sensitivity to student needs
2. Management of Teaching Situation
  a. Attention to physical condition of room
  b. Evidence of careful preparation
  c. Materials adequate and well organized
  d. Period opened promptly, students in readiness
  e. Students attentive, interested, participating
  f. Cooperativeness in teacher-student relationships
3.
The Instruction
  a. Charted toward clear objectives
  b. Methods and techniques effective
  c. Tempo suited to abilities of group
  d. Use of blackboard and other aids
  e. Optimum participation of instructor and students
  f. Clear exposition and appropriate illustrations

Excellent
Good
Fair
Inadequate
Not Evident

g. Provisions for individual dif-
    ferences
h. Accomplishment reasonable
    for period
i. Evidence of creative thought
    and work by students
j. Evidence of favorable student
    attitudes
    Remarks and Suggestions
    Signed.

The second is one made up by a faculty committee. This Committee as it pondered the problem of recommendation for salary increases, for promotions and for nonrenewal of contracts established the following criteria:

Excellent
Good
Fair
Inadequate
Not Evident

1. Teaching ability
    a. Record of successful teaching
        in previous position.
    b. Daily preparation for class
        work.
    c. Teaching procedures used.
    d. Results gained.
    e. Personal relations with stu-
        dents and colleagues.
2. Higher education
    a. Degrees held.

Excellent
Good
Fair
Inadequate
Not Evident

  b. Semester hours completed beyond highest degree.
  c. Amount of specialization to meet assignments.
  d. Recognized nonacademic training programs completed outside of colleges.
  e. Quality of scholarship demonstrated and honors won while receiving training in colleges or elsewhere.
 3. Professional productivity and leadership
  a. Publications.
   1. Books published
   2. Research projects published.
   3. Articles in learned journals.
   4. Significance or value of publications.
  b. Participation and leadership in professional organizations.
   1. Memberships in local, state and national professional associations or agencies.
   2. Committee assignments received.
   3. Scholarly addresses given.
   4. Citations or honors granted.
 4. Productivity within the University

	Not Evident	Inadequate	Fair	Good	Excellent

a. Contributions to organization and development.
b. Contributions to instructional programs.
c. Contributions to student life.

5. Outreach into the Community.
   a. Membership and leadership in community organizations.

6. Experience
   a. Total teaching experiences.
   b. Years of college experience.
   c. Creditable experiences in nonacademic institutions and agencies.
   d. Amount and kinds of experience in colleges and elsewhere which have a direct bearing upon a field of specialization.

7. Personal qualities and relationships
   a. Cultural and intellectual breadth.
   b. Personal fitness including character and wholesome influence.
   c. Acceptance by associates in the university and community.
   d. Creative ability and sound judgment.

Excellent
Good
Fair
Inadequate
Not Evident

    e. Ability to cooperate or work constructively with students, colleagues and community representatives.

  8. Ability and willingness to participate in student activities and in activities pertaining to university objectives, programs and routines.

  9. Scholarly interests, research projects, and plans for professional advancement.

I was glad to see these criteria established by the faculty itself. Any good chairman, dean or administrator charged with the responsibility of making judgements will follow, unconsciously more or less, the same general criteria. Passing judgments upon men and women is always a trying task. A conscientious administrator will work at the problem and try to make decisions as objectively as possible. As long as they are in a person's favor, the decision will be a popular one. The trouble comes when they are not favorable. Is there any rational solution? None, except that conscientious administrators out of reach of vindictive vested interests will work assiduously and honestly to build an outstanding faculty to serve the students.

6

GUIDANCE OF STUDENTS

A COMMERCIAL OR PROPRIETARY INSTITUTION USUALLY HAS a specific course and is concerned solely with instruction. Anything beyond this is simply an added attraction to enroll more students. Unfortunately, there are many in the academic field who share the same point of view perhaps without realizing it. They use as an historical justification that the universities of old were involved only with the teaching of subjects. Anything beyond that basic responsibility is fol-de-rol. I maintain that guidance is something that should permeate the whole institution. It should start before the student goes to a college, and it should continue long after he leaves. It should include the student's development as a social individual, as a citizen, as a worker in society. Anything less is shortchanging the student unless the point of view is clearly stated in the catalogue. The spirit of guidance should permeate the entire faculty, the office staff, and even the custodial staff. Just because this idea is so intertwined in everything that happens in a college, it is difficult to discuss it solely in this chapter and references to various aspects occur in other chapters.

A great deal of guidance occurs during the year preceding admission, I am purposely omitting a chapter on promotion because promotion in its true professional sense is nothing more than the dissemination of correct information and the giving of good guidance. All the rest is simply mechanics of organization. The object of promotion on the part of a college is to see to it that the institution serves those students who stand to gain by attending the institution. It must seek to give to prospective students and to their parents a clear picture of how it can contribute to their growth.

Promotion involves four possibilities:

1. mailed literature; 2. talks at high schools; 3. functions or mass conferences at the college which prospective students can attend, and 4. a personal interview either at the high school or at the college.

It is as simple as that. Personal interviews at the college are to my mind the most important. They should be conducted on a high professional level. The purpose is not to acquire a student, but to see whether the college can help the student. In some cases the student may have to be discouraged from going to college. In other cases, some other institution may better fit his or her need. In other words, the college interview complements the high school guidance.

Once the student is in college, the college has to be concerned with academic progress, physical and social development and over-all guidance toward a life career. It is to be regretted that often some college officers limit themselves to the first concern—and then take action only when the harm has been done. There are two things that seem to me fundamental. First, students should be tested in reading ability. Reading ability is not solely a matter of native intelligence. It is a matter of habit and unfortunately people have been reading less and less ever since radio and television were developed. Television has, of course, done away with most of the slight efforts to browse through any form of reading matter. I think the issue is clear. Either we close our doors to all but the top five percent of prospects or else we have to buckle down and teach an appreciable number of students how to read. It seems to me that reading ability is so basic to success in college we can not afford to sidestep the issue. It means testing the students at the outset of their collegiate career; it means special classes; it means extra expense and the disturbance of an orderly sequence of English courses in the usual curriculum.

The other matter closely allied to reading is orientation and guidance in studying habits. Some good instructors will be doing this naturally along with their teaching. Most, however, just take it for granted that students know how to study efficiently and in this they are as wrong as they can be. Guidance means in its barest essence, helping the student to come out of his shell. One never knows when a student is going to find inspiration and spread his wings. The college should offer as many opportunities as possible for young people not only to go to concerts, plays, operas, and art exhibits, but also to go on factory visits, sight-seeing tours, observations of institutions and communities.

These out-of-class projects don't necessarily have to be related to the subject. Even if an instructor says "Next week, we're going to have a picnic," or "My hobby is flowers. I'm inviting you to go to the flower show with me," he's going to add to the total of college experiences. Young people, for all their wild talk, are essentially the same people we were in our youth. They want companionship; they enjoy doing and seeing things with other people.

Guidance includes outside speakers in the classroom. A fresh point of view is going to reach some of the young people, and who knows what lifetime results may come from such a discussion. But all of these things boil down to mechanics and attention to details. They should all be part of an instructor's pattern of activities. And it's good for instructors too! It takes them out of the deadening effect of sameness, and gives their teaching a lift.

In all of this faculty-student relationship, everything depends on the point of view. If we think of the college as a sort of subject matter cafeteria where each student is served a plate of English, another one of mathematics, and another of French, all to be partaken of by the young people with varying degrees of digestibility, than all these other matters are of no concern. But, if we think of the college period as a process of maturing in which the subjects play a part, but in which many other factors are involved, then it behooves the administrative officers to look for other concomitants. For instance, whether the institution is a boarding one or not, the social contact between faculty and students is important. I believe that each instructor ought to invite a group of students to a social gathering once a semester or so, preferably at his home, but if not, in a college reception room. At our college, I used to have each instructor concentrate on his advisees. Reasonable expenses for refreshments were paid for by the college. Some instructors will be more adept at this than others. But I feel strongly that these opportunities for faculty and students to know each other better are important.

Social functions at the college are important. Some

administrators believe that the students ought to be left to themselves when they have social functions. I disagree with this point of view. There should be three or four faculty couples at all functions. At the major functions, four or five times a year, all of the faculty ought to turn out. I believe there will be a much more wholesome spirit in the whole social program if the faculty and students are together. It is my observation that there are too many instances where students have been left to their own devices with resulting lowering of social standards and excesses of a disturbing nature.

Social development of students should be a matter of major concern by the college. All types of socializing experiences become a part of this development: trips, attendance at concerts, going to games, in short, any out-of-class activities where young people can engage in conversation. But the purely social activities are important too. As I point out elsewhere, I believe the whole faculty ought to enter into the picture of social activities. And the idea is to try to get to those students who need social experiences most. Too often, social activities are planned by the extroverts and for the extroverts only. That is why I believe strongly in square dancing where students are encouraged to come singly and become a part of the group through the evening.

What about fraternities and sororities? The development of the fraternity system is very easy to understand. During the early phases of colleges in America there were so few institutions that naturally people had to be away from home in order to attend. Boarding houses sprang up near colleges and friendships formed therein led to a desire for more formal organization. True, some colleges had dormitories but the inadequacy and the institutional character of these emphasized the value of the fraternity house.

As long as colleges were small, and as long as there were no more than eight or ten Greek letter houses on the campus, it was fairly easy for a sort of controllable social pattern to operate. Autos were few and liquor and drugs had not become the vogue in our society. The boys could stray a little but not too far nor too long. Besides, fraternity houses relieved the college administration of much of the necessity for dormitory and feeding arrangments, and that was a blessing indeed. As our colleges increased, the good qualities of the fraternity system tended to be minimized and the wrong qualities emphasized. As the institution began to spread all over town, control became well-nigh impossible. While on one hand there developed a socially exclusive group, there grew outside the fraternities a large socially undigested group of students which became a problem. You will notice that institutions that have unlimited funds are trying to de-emphasize the fraternity system by bringing it under greater college control and by building up units within the college that are socially and intellectually controllable. Unfortunately, most colleges don't have the money for these expensive undertakings. Fortunately for the small college, more can be done to alleviate these conditions than in a large, sprawling institution.

In too many cases, as far as the fraternities are concerned, the tail is wagging the dog. It's the fraternity first, the college second. Too many alumni have an immature attitude toward the whole matter and still believe the college is a place for the development of swashbuckling gay Lotharios with the fraternity house as the base of operation.

What are the common criticisms of fraternities? They are too snobbish? Let the college therefore seek to democratize the social relationships existing within the college, and this means having a special program that is college centered with the fraternities in a secondary role. Fraternities emphasize the wrong values? Let the faculty have it definitely understood that scholarship and service are to be emphasized. And let there be no question of how lapses in social mores will be dealt with. But the president or the dean cannot do it alone. It must be a concerted move on the part of the faculty, trustees, and even parents. Pump priming in the form of regulatory devices may be necessary, but from the long view range it means a sound, all-inclusive and sympathetic program of social development.

Today, the fraternity system has been de-emphasized at many institutions for a number of reasons: students are older and more mature, many are married, the co-educational scene, the taking over by the college of the boarding and housing. Along with the social and personality development, it also behooves a college to guide the student towards life work. Here, of course, we find a cleavage in academic circles. Should a college think simply in terms of intellectual development or should it concentrate on life career objectives. I don't think it is necessary to get into this debate at this time. I happen to think that a college should do both but, regardless of whether a college is a straight liberal arts institution or not, I do feel strongly that guidance for life work must be given somehow in college, and it should be given from the very first year. If the college philosophy is that pure arts and sciences can be a suitable background for any life career, then it must bear out its premise by showing just how this philosophy works out. Is a major simply an intellectual field of endeavor with no practical application, or is it a straight road to a career? The student should be guided into an understanding of the relationship of his studies of his life.

Possible military service, or a year off working or traveling "to find one's self" tend to make it imperative for students to think of what to do with their lives. Young men and women are getting married during the late teens and the early twenties. The married student with a child or two is a permanent part of the academic picture. It seems to me that we are professionally bound to give students maximum guidance toward careers, to provide placement service, and to continue this service as far as possible after graduation.

Lastly, what about spiritual values? I certainly would agree that therein lies the greatest failure of colleges. Furthermore, I don't see how most colleges, unless they are limited to a sectarian student body, can achieve very much along this line. If the institution is nonsectarian then it must tread gingerly on the whole religious question lest it be accused of sponsoring doctrines or ideas contrary to those of some of its students. Even if it is sectarian it is bound to have many students of other faiths and it is faced with almost the same problem. In the early days of higher education in America, there was a relative religious homogeneity in our colleges and the spiritual element was an integral part of college activities. With the advent of the tax-supported institution and the heterogeneous character of most institutions, the religious side of colleges has become practically a thing of the past. But some things can be done, especially in the smaller institutions. Certainly the institution can encourage each student to become a firmer adherent of his own faith. Character training can be a function of the guidance of the college, and again may I stress that it has to be an over-all picture with everyone cooperating. Character and personality and spiritual upbringing are interrelated and each one merges with and influences the other. Each instructor in his classroom and in out-of-class activities should have just as much responsibility in this direction as a college chaplain. A spirit of charity, of consideration for others, of helpfulness to people and to causes—this can be inculcated in students in a small college. And most important, the faculty must set the example and establish the tone of the institution.

7

FUND RAISING

THE COLLEGE PRESIDENT IS SUPPOSED TO BE CHOSEN FOR scholarly achievement or administrative ability, but usually fund raising is one of his chores. A few presidents really relish the job; most dislike it. Generally speaking, I believe it is unfortunate that presidents have to spend so much time in fund raising, but, since it must be done, the best thing to do is to decide how much can be done and the most efficient way of doing it.

First of all, it is necessary to survey the field and to decide the area to be covered. There are four possible sources of contributions to the college:

1. Alumni
2. Community—individuals and industries
3. Foundations
4. Legislative bodies and government agencies

The alumni are discussed more fully in another chapter. Their contributions are going to depend on a number of factors: first, the age and the traditions of the institution; second, the economic background of the alumni; and third, the efforts put forth by the college to solicit their help. The great gifts we hear about are most often given on purely sentimental grounds. With the exception of a few institutions, the great mass of alumni solicitation is a laborious process and often does not meet the cost of raising the funds. In many cases, the expense of raising the money is charged to other activities. The time expended by the president or other members is never taken into consideration. I know of one fairly large university that just doesn't bother with alumni, financially or otherwise. And yet, alumni solicitation is necessary because if it does nothing else, it at least helps the alumni association to meet some of its own expense.

Fund raising naturally is tied up with public relations. Doesn't it boil down to two things: first, to describe to the alumni and community the real services of the college, and second, to point up the specific needs of the institution?

Believe it or not, one of the most difficult things for an older person to do, if he or she has any money, is to decide how to give it away. If there are children, the problem is more or less easily solved. But there are many people who have no natural heirs, or who are estranged from their sons and daughters or who are not particularly fond of their relatives. A small college can present a good case. To give you an example: we had a part time cleaning woman who left $5,000 to the library and $25,000 to our cultural center in Rutherford. I believe a prospective donor will be attracted best by a worthwhile memorial to him or to her that serves an important need. People do want to be remembered; those who give anonymously are in the small minority.

Therefore let the president, with the help of his faculty, make up a list of worthy projects varying these in amounts to fit all types of donors. But, and this increasingly is necessary, make sure that a portion of such a gift is in the form of endowment whose income will maintain it.

The second best possbility is the establishment of scholarships for needy students, such scholarships bearing the donor's name.

Everything else is a poor third.

The first mechanical task is to make out a good list of individuals and companies in the community that may be of help. Start with a list of twenty or fifty or a hundred real friends of the college and have them make suggestions. This can best be done by a personal visit. Industrial indices, phone books or chamber of commerce lists can help to supplement the list. Faculty, students, and alumni can add to it. This address list should be circularized from time to time with interesting news from the college.

This list is extremely important and has to be combed once or twice a year by the fund raising person and by the president. One thing that happens especially as a college becomes larger is that lackadaisical employees let these lists go out of date. Another waste of energy is that perpetrated by a new fund raising director who just buries everything of the past and has to start anew. It is important to watch carefully undelivered mail and make a note quickly of changes of names and address and of deaths. The smaller the institution, the more the president has to be on top of the procedures in fund raising.

A foundation screening service may be of help. Many appeals to foundations are duplicative and the letters can be made automatically on the special typewriters changing the introduction and perhaps the ending. But the president has to pump prime the procedure and the fund raising person and his assistants have to know that the president knows and cares about fund raising. Most of these foundations have pet charities, and others will not be interested in the small college. But there may be one out of one hundred that may become interested in some project of the college or in special scholarships. There again, it's a matter of deciding how much time one can afford to devote to this purpose.

I am omitting any discussion of means of raising funds from legislative bodies and government agencies. This would require a tome by itself and has so many diverse factors that it is inadvisable to include it in this book.

Recently, in many states there have been united college drives. Private institutions have banded together and, in addition to their own drives, are conducting a cooperative appeal. The central office will have a staff including a director, and the appeals go out to all companies within the state. Many companies which would not attempt to pick out any particular college for their benefactions are willing to contribute to a state-wide drive. Each college has the right as a rule to request that certain companies not be approached because they are contributing to the particular institution. Generally, half of the money collected is divided equally, the other half according to enrollment. Expenses are shared similarly. Each state group has a somewhat different structure, of course. Teams of two college representatives, one of whom is usually a college president, do the personal solicitation. The average time given seems to be about twenty days out of the year. In some states, the colleges have been successful in bringing into active participation leading industrialists who are effective in soliciting their colleagues.

There is an added factor involved. There is a movement on foot whereby companies having centers of operation all over the country contribute to a national fund, the money thus collected to be shared by those states having statewide funds. Here again, the president of a private institution must decide what is best for his college and how much time he can devote to the enterprise.

Another potential source of financial help to colleges is the annuity plan which is not new, but has been blessed with particular advantages recently because of the tax laws. Under this plan, a donor gives a certain sum of money to the college, which in turn gives him a yearly income for life. This income can be based on one of two general plans. The first is to guarantee a certain rate of interest, ranging from perhaps five to nine percent, according to age. The less his life expectancy, the greater is the percentage. Some institutions will take a chance and give even a greater percentage, and in some cases they have found themselves paying out more than they eventually receive. Generally this happens when an institution needs money badly and is ready to mortgage its future in order to get ready cash. Colleges have been getting more conservative and are basing their annuity on mortality tables, their highest percentage rarely exceeding the highest income they, themselves, can realize on the principal. The recent high interest rates, however, have diminished the attractiveness of such plans and it may be necessary to offer higher inducements to annuitants than would usually be the case.

The other plan is to base the return to the donor on

the actual income rate of the endowment fund of the college. In other words, the college really invests the money for the individual and pays to him whatever the investment makes. On his death, the college gets the principal.

There are two advantages for the donor. First, part of the principal involved is considered a contribution and therefore tax exempt up to twenty per cent of total income. Second, part of his income may be considered tax exempt. There are so many variants and possibilities that it would be foolhardy to go into the subject at length, particularly when laws change from year to year. But, the general idea is that the actual yearly return from the college, plus the tax advantages, equal if not surpass the annuity rates of insurance companies. The plan works better with persons who have above average incomes. There is also the possibility that a person, instead of giving cash, may give stocks, bonds or real estate and thus avoid a capital gains tax on profits in most cases. Income is then figured on the value of the gift on the date it was made.

Here again the president is faced with a problem of what he should do. My personal feelings are that while such an annuity plan means extra work, there are substantial financial advantages to the college. I would advise two things: not to use the principal of the gift until the donor has passed away, and second, to base the percentage paid to the donor on a rate not higher than the foreseeable average income from the invested funds.

In all of this fund raising activity, the inevitable question arises as to the advisability of using professional fund raisers. Some small colleges are fortunate in having a good development director. The trouble is that if the person is good, he will soon be looking for a more lucrative position with a large institution. Should the president try to do it all as is done in some institutions? I'm afraid no one has the answer to this question. Certain it is that whatever time is put in on fund raising must be taken away from educational leadership. The bringing in of a commercial fund raising concern does not solve the problem. The company does not do the fund raising. It surveys the field; it plans, organizes and directs. If the money isn't there to begin with, it won't be able to manufacture donors. It can only help the president do what he doesn't find time or is loathe to do. But in the end, the president will be inexorably led by the company to put in the time necessary.

There is no magic in fund raising concerns. They'll simply drill wells, methodically and efficiently, for the oil to gush forth. But if there isn't any oil, none will come forth. And companies are expensive and very often college executives will find it very irritating that the fund raising people are getting more compensation than any member of the faculty, including themselves. Moreover, one only hears of the successful drives. Neither the company nor the college will talk about failures. It is very evident that figures are often padded. Otherwise, how could an institiution raise hundreds of thousands for endowments or capital improvements, and not have it show in either category. Let's face it, out of 3,000 institutions of higher learning, probably not more than 200 are really striking pay dirt. Let us not be led astray by glib convention speakers. And where is the big money going to? It mainly goes to the old established institutions who have had a chance to build up rich alumni. Once in a while a generous donor will contribute a few millions to a new local institution.

My advice is that a college president should devote about twenty per cent of his time to fund raising. I believe he should have a reliable company or individual make an objective survey of the fund raising possibilities every five years or so. If the possibilities exist, then there ought to be concentrated drives periodically for specific purposes. I believe that in many cases it is well to use a reliable fund raising concern for this purpose. There ought to be an annual giving campaign among the alumni. There should be someone on the permanent college staff who will keep on developing fund-raising possibilities. The president will probably find that he has to be the real leader. He can't just dump it in the lap of a staff member. But something has to be done each week. Set up the office mechanics so that records will be clear and up-to-date. And, don't forget to write letters of thanks to donors. There will be discouraging moments. The prospect from whom you expected $10,000 will give you $100. The only thing you can do is to thank him for his thoughtful gift. The Lord will undoubtedly even up matters by providing a larger gift from sources you never expected.

I believe the president ought to cultivate a number of prospective donors including heads of large corporations and banking executives and lawyers who specialize in wills. How many should he handle? My suggestion is one per week. Because I wanted to save time, I used to have simple lunches in my office. This saved me about forty minutes driving to the country club. But I found that my guests enjoyed the simple lunches in my office. I would offer a glass of sherry and while my secretary prepared things so that I could take over with a proper flourish I would either have an omelette or a hamburger which I prepared myself plus a salad and a simple dessert like a fruit yogurt with a biscuit. I enjoyed and my guests enjoyed the spartan but genuine hospitality. No interruptions were allowed and talking was easy and informal. Most of the important gifts came from these sessions. To this very day, these persons have remained friends. Easy does it—and sincerity.

In my lifetime of experience, I have seen the following misuse of opportunities:

1. lack of communication between the fund raising and the other departments of the college
2. lack of simplicity. Too many people involved in doing the same thing with the result that with a multiplicity of crossmemoranda, the result is nonproductive and expensive confusion.
3. prospects are invited but no one knows them or greets them and the guest is left stranded.
4. prospects are invited but there is no follow through. In other words, no one ever gets to the all-important sales pitch.
5. lack of proper publicity.

I think every administrator and an appreciable number of faculty members ought to be involved in fund raising and encouragement ought to be given in this respect. As a matter of fact, very often, large gifts come in because of the personal interests of an administrator or a professor. True in practically every case, it is a matter of building his or her own preserve. But it's all part of building an institution. If a science professor gets money for a laboratory or for conducting an experiment, this is all part of the overall picture. I suggest a cadre of about fifty per cent of the total adminstrative and faculty staff to be trained to try for contributions or grants. From time to time there might be a faculty session on how to secure contributions and grants, with the successful ones teling how they did it. It may spur others who then might be able to expand their professional activities.

In conclusion, I should like to reiterate that fund raising is an activity that must be led by the president. Nonproductive sideshows and time-wasting cosmetic effects should be avoided. The emphasis has to be on getting dollars for worthwhile activities and there has to be a basic sincerity operating. It is not a case of getting money just to make a job for someone or to create something that is unneeded. Operations should be basically simple so that it is easy to see at a glance what is being accomplished. It should be made clear that whoever is working for fund raising realizes that he or she has to produce. Above all, records should be kept accurately that can be easily passed on to the next crew. There is apt to be more turnover in fund-raising offices than in other departments. The system should be such that continuity can easily operate and that valuable contacts are not forgotten or lost. Fund raising is a continuous common sense activity combining a lot of hard work and drudgery with creative effort.

8

ALUMNI

ONE DEAN I SPOKE TO SAID THAT AT HIS COLLEGE THEY JUST didn't bother with alumni. It wasn't worth the trouble. In another institution, it almost seemed as if the college did nothing but stir up alumni activity. Everything else was of secondary importance. Alumni activity takes energy; again the president must decide on a pattern. How much of his time should be given to alumni; how much of the college's resources can be devoted to alumni work? What should he be trying to accomplish? Is it merely fund raising?

The first thing that has to be checked is the purely mechanical organization for alumni follow-up. The addressing machine stencils have to be kept up to date, and it takes time and money to do it. We assume that there is a part time or full time secretary. Once every year, there ought to be a mail check-up to find out changes in jobs, marital status, and other pertinent facts. I feel that colleges have a moral obligation to have a general idea of what their alumni are doing.

We in academic circles take things too much for

granted. Our curricular patterns are sometimes established by intelligent planning, but far too often they are
the result of chance and of the pressure of vested interests within the college. We should be able to say that as
a result of going to college, alumni are better professional persons, or better members of society or better
family men and women. Is a college education simply a
social asset based on snob appeal? Is it simply an in-
nocuous period of one's life spent in idyllic surround-
ings until the problems of living smack the student
squarely in the face? I believe strongly that a college
ought to evaluate its work through the alumni periodically. It ought to try to find out first of all whether its
objectives are being reached or whether they ought to
be changed.

➤ The alumni magazine is another matter of expense.
Keeping in mind the small institution of two thousand
or less, it is my thought that there ought to be about
three issues a year with at least sixteen pages in each
issue. Since the magazine is going to compete with
many other more flamboyant commercial magazines
and advertising organs, the articles ought to be short
and the illustrations plentiful. Watch out for the alumnus or the faculty member who believes that the only
purpose of the alumni magazine is to run lengthy articles about his pet theories. I believe strongly that the
main purpose of an alumni magazine is to enable the
alumnus to keep abreast of the developments at the
college and to have an appreciation of the institution's
service to the community in the larger sense.

It seems to me almost pointless to have a magazine
and not send it to all alumni. If the college sends it only
to subscribers, it reaches the ones who need the
stimulus the least and omits the stray sheep who should
be encouraged back into the fold.

A word about getting out the magazine might be in

order. We assume that for two or three months, items of interest have been put in a folder and perhaps three or four commissioned articles are ready. The time comes to put the magazine together. I don't see why it should take more than two days of concentrated work to whip the thing into shape. Get a printer who will cooperate in getting the galleys, the final proof, and the magazine printed quickly. When the galleys come in, make up the dummy that day. If everything goes well, the final proof can be approved over the phone. I emphasize these mechanical details because the matter of time and expense is so important with a small college. Planned efficiently, the cost of the magazine can be kept down. If you don't watch this process, the editor will spawn an assistant editor, both will cry for secretaries, endless "editorial conferences" will evolve, the multiplicity of staff plus probably student part time workers will build up an expensive empire. A small college can't afford costly bureaucratic structures. Once the magazine is printed, it should go out immediately, again a matter of planning the mechanical details.

One last suggestion: the magazine ought to be large enough and its cover attractive enough so the alumni will want to keep it and show it to their friends. An attractive format will be good public relations for the college and will be an invitation to read.

It is important, of course, to keep good records of graduates. The first step is to make sure lists are in order. These have to be combed and recombed. Titles, spelling, addresses have to be correct. Today, much of this can be computerized, but I have seen cases where the attitude was to leave it all to the computer. It is well to keep in mind the old saying about computers: "Garbage in, garbage out." Incidentally, the computer ought to be able to sort out names and addresses of alumni:

by class
by curriculum
geographically
by employer
husband and wife both graduates
contributors
class agents
sons and daughter of former graduates

A decision has to be made on what to charge for alumni dues if any, and whether the dues increase with the years. Then begins the laborious process of trying to find out which alumni have the possibility of giving substantial sums, which ones can prevail on members of their families or companies, or foundations, which ones can make good class agents. But it is also important to know which alumni can be of help in recommending applicants for admission.

The problem of how to entice the alumni to revisit the college will vary according to the type of college. If the alumni are spread all over the United States, one should, of course, concentrate on the yearly homecoming with all its attendant headaches. Athletics and heavy drinking seem to be inextricably woven into these traditional festivities. Like everything else, the success of these gatherings takes it toll in time and energy. I believe I would be correct in saying that institutions want their alumni to come back and want them to enjoy themselves, but that they want these meetings to be more sober alumni sessions where some serious talking can take place and where some fund-raising organizing can be accomplished. I feel strongly also that whatever arrangements are made ought to be made with husbands and wives in mind.

This last point brings up a very important aspect of alumni organization. For an institution whose alumni are within easy access, there is a splendid opportunity to help young couples enjoy a joint interest. It doesn't matter whether the husband or the wife is the graduate. Let them both partiicipate in alumni doings. For one thing, it increases the number of people interested in the college. But there is a more important issue involved. If we agree that one of the objectives of good education is to create a stronger family group, then this is an opportunity to implement the idea. At our college we have held to the idea that the institution is to serve as a permanent center of activities for the alumni. The library is at their disposal, and we put in whatever books they would like. A few years ago, for instance, we observed that quite a few of our alumni were building their own homes. Therefore, we put in scores of books on every phase of small house building, including interior decoration. Our placement bureau is always at their service. Through the years we have helped the alumni plan a series of functions held at the college at very reasonable cost. In addition, they receive various notices throughout the year of dramatic and musical productions. Our campuses are small enough so that the mechanics involved are not complicated. But in all of this the president of a small institution is faced with the necessity of helping to decide what is going to be the sphere of alumni activity. In most cases, the directing alumni group will need help, otherwise three weaknesses may develop:

1. The members may get bogged down in details.
2. Being inexperienced they may simply do nothing.
3. Someone within the group will sway them toward unsound tangents.

This does not mean that we don't want to encourage

the alumni to be as self-sufficient as possible and to have a democratic organization. It simply means that the college can be a sort of continuing agent for a richer and more efficient alumni program.

Different presidents do different things to encourage alumni interest. At one institution, the president writes a card to each graduate every year upon his birthday. At another, the president writes a letter every time a marriage or engagement clipping comes in. I like to invite groups of twenty or thirty alumni to my home to talk about themselves and about the college.

Now the question comes up as to what part the alumni should play in the running of an institution. Certainly we can deplore the undue influence of alumni in athletic matters. On the other hand, I believe it makes sense to listen to what the alumni have to say, not just one or two vociferous ones or just those who may have pet ideas, but to get a sampling of opinions of various groups. Some good ideas are bound to come out. The ultimate and full responsibility for the objectives and the instruction must rest with the faulty and the trustees. Alumni are in a sense part of the larger community and as such the president should have his ears attuned to their thoughts. Alumni acquire the right to have a stronger voice as they serve the institution, as they acquire a sense of educational values, as they become familiar with the problems facing the college.

9

PARENTS

EACH COLLEGE PRESIDENT WILL HAVE HIS OWN IDEAS ABOUT parents. One person I knew didn't want to have anything at all to do with parents because he felt they complicated his existence and were a potential source of disturbance. Others have gone to the other extreme and have used parents as a buffer between the students and the administration. I believe there is a sensible and reasonable middle course. After all, in most cases, the parents are paying the bills. They should not be frozen out. At the same time, we do not want to get the parents in the frame of mind that every time Bobby's aunt comes in for a visit, Mommy calls up prexy for a special absence pass. But let us remember that the mother whose boy or girl is going to college is going through one of the most difficult adjustments in life. And, if it's a boy, the fact that he may be considering military service or a year off to travel or acquire life experience doesn't make the adjustment any easier for the family.

But now a new factor has been added. The enormous

cost of a college education has exacerbated the financial problem. Some parents have actually had to take a second mortgage in order to pay for the tuition bills. Naturally parents have a right to know whether they are receiving value for the fortunes they are expending.

What can we do for parents? First, parents want to know as much as possible about the college. Students will usually give them little information. They could, of course, write long weekly letters reporting all the tidbits, but usually they won't unless it happens to be money-asking time. It might be well for the president or someone in the college to prepare a parents' letter three or four times a year. It doesn't have to be more than a xeroxed affair. Certain of our parents have asked to subscribe to the college newspaper. Since student newspapers often give a skewed view of a college, this may be counterproductive. We set up the parents' listings on our addressograph at registration time so that the problem of circularizing the parents became fairly easy. Thus, they can also be circularized for special events, such as the college dramatic productions or concerts.

The second thing we must do for the parents is to arrange certain days during the year when they will be encouraged to visit the college. The entire faculty should be on hand and there should be as much activity as possible. The library, the laboratories, the offices, should be open. All this is elementary, but it is surprising to note that not all colleges do this. Furthermore, I believe that it might be well for the president to give a brief talk on some of the things the college is doing or trying to do. The talk may be repetitious from year to year, but can be varied, and whatever is said will be absorbed hungrily by most parents. Does this seem too "high schoolish"? Not at all. This is the sort of thing a small college can do.

Third, there can be special events for certain groups of parents. This will vary with the type of institution. Some women's colleges have a father and daughter weekend when papa can have the undisputed attention of his daughter for a few days. Mothers are definitely not encouraged to tag along. Dad is kingpin for a day or two and does he love it! As far as I know, there are no mother-son days at any of the colleges. But you do have father-son banquets and mother-daughter teas or dinners. They all serve good purposes. Their success depends on the energetic drive of the person handling the function. But the understanding appreciation of prexy, can do much to encourage the staff member in charge.

I found that a Parents' Council of fifty members was of great help to me as a sounding board. The group was made up democratically. When students registered they could propose their parents for membership, father or mother or both. These were accepted automatically. Remaining vacancies were filled by nomination from the faculty. The Parents' Council met once a semester. We would have discussions on many different topics: institutional matters, guidance, social affairs, dress standards, marriage clinic, study habits, and many other subjects. During the evening, there would be closed ballot votes on various questions and the results read publicly. I have derived a great deal of support on many matters. While it is true that the trustees and faculty will make certain decisions, it is also comforting to be able to have the official approbation of the parents' representatives. For instance, we were toying with the idea of having students participate in the investing of endowment funds, under expert guidance, of course. When we started we were anxious to discuss the idea with various groups, and it was very encouraging to have a strong approbation of parents. Naturally, a parents' council is only possible when parents can reach the institution easily.

I like parents. I feel keenly the sacrifice most of them are making to send their sons and daughters to college. The college can be a source of strength to the parents who, after all, are an important part of the community. Why doesn't it make sense for parents and their children to strengthen their relationship on a mature level during the college period? Why should it be a period of weakening ties? Why can't the college be a bond between the parents and the students?

Let us not forget that parents can help out in fund raising, and that a certain number of them will be potential givers. I dislike very much putting pressure on parents for that purpose. I believe that any appeals, ought to be very tactfully worded. Many will give good leads and will do a great deal of the spade work. It is good for them to realize that a college can not exist on tuition alone. Even if a parent can not contribute anything he or she is going to have a better concept of the costly services a college offers.

Some of our parents have been of enormous help in other ways. One of them was instrumental in getting us started on our archives. Another one financed the organizing of our horse riding project which now includes 120 other institutions. Another one was of enormous help in the investment of funds. Another one helped to set up our Town and Gown Society. Still another one was responsible for a work-study plan. Another helped on our business curriculum. If you study your admission applications, you'll find a wealth of possible helpers. Some parents have become lifelong friends. Just a few weeks ago, a striking young lady came to see me at my home. She was the new editor of the college newspaper. "You don't know me but my mother was one of your first graduates. I'd like to interview you and have you reminisce about the early days." At my age, what could be more fun? Which brings up another point: alumni are prospective parents and this is important for the continuity of the college.

10

FOOD SERVICE

LET US REMEMBER THAT WE'RE CONCERNED WITH THE SMALL institution of two thousand or less. Whether the college is a boarding one or not, food service will always be a thorny problem. It will probably be the greatest single source of student irritation. No matter how good it is, there will always be grumbling. This is to be expected. When people eat in the same institution, whether it be an Army camp or the Waldorf Astoria, they are going to get tired of the sameness and, besides, no one can plan meals that are going to please everybody. So the college president might just as well inure himself to a certain amount of grousing.

But he also might just as well learn something about food so that he can direct intelligently what has to be done. It will pay dividends to the institution and dividends to his peace of mind. He may be lucky enough to have a good director of food service. But if he hasn't or if he or she leaves, he's going to be faced with a real problem. Moreover, if he doesn't watch out, there is the danger that a sizeable deficit will develop. This will be the department in the college that will need the greatest control because the chances for wastage, pilfering, carelessness, and downright dishonesty are endless. If you have a good person in charge, he or she will appreciate having someone above who knows the difficulties involved and who can lend a helping hand at the right moment.

Some institutions avail themselves of a service company that takes over the whole problem. There are some very good ones in the field and they try to do a good job. They operate on various principles. In some cases, the institution pays the deficit or gets the profit, if there is one. In other cases, they may charge a certain percentage of the gross. In any event, these concerns are not in business for their health, and one can rest assured that the institution is not going to get any bargains. Whatever the arrangement is, it's not going to solve all the problems.

What are the disadvantages? First, they have a help problem. The small institution will get the lesser or the younger managers. As these managers get experience and become more ambitious, they have to be moved upward to larger institutions or industrial concerns where they can get larger salaries. The result is that the small institution has almost a yearly turnover. You can not buy continuity from these companies. Generally speaking, although there are exceptions, they will lack imagination. The small institution will not get the top notch manager or chef. Sum up this question by saying that such a company will help you on some of the problems, but that it will need your active guidance just the same. I would also say that, in spite of its claims, it will be more expensive than if you operated things yourself

efficiently, but less expensive than if you were to operate your food service inefficiently.

One advantage of a service is that it may help you in
arranging public dinners. An active institution will find
it necessary to have any number of these serving fifteen
to five hundred people. A good company takes over the
whole problem. It usually can bring in extra chefs and
waitresses and follow through; if a college is in a relatively isolated region, it may not even be able to do this.
But you still will have to specify what you want. You
might just as well plan five or six standard menus and
standardize the whole process. With the person in
charge, decide what you will charge and simplify
things. Good public relations require that you have
these facilities available and these meals have to be
done well or not at all.

What about liquor? In the case of church-related institutions with strict teetotal principles, the problem is
solved—no liquor. But today in most institutions, cock-
tails are *de rigueur*. Again the president has to make
decisions; sometimes it may be necessary to have the
trustees involved in setting basic principles. Open bars
with their inevitable wastage and leftover problems
seems to become more and more the norm. I know of
one institution where when it was figured out what the
open bar cost, it came to five drinks per person, which
was unlikely. Only two thirds of the people drank and
then most had one drink. An open bar leads to pilferage
and wastage. I think it makes much more sense to have
domestic sherry or wine, if you wish to have something
special, domestic champagne. I still have to have a great
many receptions and I find that the latter costs far less
and is easier to handle than open bar. It seems strange
to have to discuss liquor in an academic book but, as

president, you might just as well decide to do whatever has to be done, with verve and with sophistication.

I believe that the president ought to know the fundamentals of nutrition. The necessary elements can be learned in an hour. I have found that these catering organizations pay little attention to nutrition because they operate on a commercial basis. Their idea is to raise the gross and make the student spend as much as possible when a cafeteria is being operated. The point of view of the college should be different. We are not interested in making the student spend a great deal. We want him to get proper nourishment at the least possible cost. We want to make sure that there are always enough good items at low cost.

I know you will think I am paying too much attention to nutrition, but you can't pay enough attention to nutrition. You are involved with a moral principle. Proper eating is just as important a part of the college cirriculum as physical training or intellectual discipline. Some colleges have given up on this problem and provided student kitchens. My observation after studying about twenty colleges using this plan is negative. A few students imbued with the principles of good nutrition profit from it. The great majority acquire poor eating habits, with desultory meals and a reliance on outside fast foods, fried chicken and pizza and cake.

I believe it is well to have a student committee to pass on to you student reactions, although you can be sure that you won't be able to make everybody happy. It might be well, from time to time, to explain your posture in a parents' letter. It is also of value every once in a while to get into the cafeteria line and eat the way students do. It will be a signal to the dining room staff that you care. There may be a certain amount of stiffness on the part of the students, but they too will realize that you are watching out for them. Make mental notes (too much fooling around by kitchen staff, dirty dishes not cleared away, devastating rock music, unclean floors, etc.) and then act on them immediately.

I feel strongly that students ought to be encouraged to eat as much raw fruit and vegetables as possible so that they may get the enzymes necessary for proper digestion. Therefore, fresh fruit and attractive salads should always be featured. The easiest thing in the world is to encourage people to eat sugar-laden desserts and this goes for de luxe restaurants as well. If you disagree, try an experiment on yourself: for one month, omit as much sugar, salt and white flour as possible. Try to eat mostly raw fruit and vegetables. And then see how you feel. But if you feel better, as I know you will, if you feel that you are getting to know the secret of life, then does it not behoove you to pass on this magical secret to your students?

Whether a college has a company operating the food service or its own director, there are a few suggestions that may be useful:

1. In order to break up the feeling of uniformity, plan your meals on an eight, nine or ten day basis. It will help make people feel that every week is different.
2. I believe a college has a moral obligation to give guidance in nutrition, especially if it is a boarding institution.
3. Plenty of good bread should be provided, even if the institution has to bake it or have it baked especially.
4. Forceful direction has to be given in eating manners to the younger generation, otherwise students tend to get more informal every day.
5. Have a good system for checking expenses and

income. Perhaps one of your staff can do the auditing weekly. Proceed on the principle that you don't trust anyone when it comes to handling money in the food service. I have seen motherly women succumb to temptation. Have a clear cut system just as a bank does. And watch out that roast beefs and hams don't get into the habit of disappearing.

6. Maintain your equipment in good shape and insist on absolute neatness and cleanliness in the kitchen. Compliment the staff when things are in good order.

7. Make sure that the faculty has a good place to eat in quiet. Of course you may take the point of view that faculty and students should fraternize. That has its points. What it really means is that you are giving the faculty an extra job during meals, that of supervising the students. Generally speaking, it is my feeling that the faculty members ought to have a place to eat where they can forget the problems of the classroom.

Food service will include the refreshment for student parties. This is an important part of student activities and it should be encouraged. It should be part of the college's guidance, and it represents opportunities for students' social maturing. Someone has to be in charge of this phase and the good service director may not always be the person to do it. It can be a faculty wife or perhaps a member of the office staff who can do this as an extra activity with extra compensation. It has to be someone with a flair for efficient planning, creative ideas, and a sense of budgeting. Such a person has to know how to work with students. Activities will encompass everything from cookies and punch to a six course dinner. The great problem is going to be to allow the students as much freedom as possible and yet prevent them from making expensive errors. The easiest thing to do is to have the person in charge figure out seven or eight typical parties and work out a reasonable cost. Then you have a set of patterns. Each college has to work out its own practices. I would caution against students who have a distorted concept of how to spend somebody else's money. Unless students are given some guidance, they will never learn. It is a disservice to them to allow them to acquire habits of loose spending.

Functions for outside guests are another phase of the food service. Some colleges simply use a town restaurant or hotel. Like most things in life, there are advantages and disadvantages in any plan that is used. I personally believe that a function held within the college provides the best opportunity for public relations. Again the president must decide how much time and energy can be funneled into this activity. But these functions should be carefully planned. After all, if you are inviting a group of executives whose time is valuable, you can not give them an inferior dinner. It has to be comparable to a good dinner served in the best hotel.

All of this means that in the small college the president has to know something about food service. Even if he or she is lucky enough to have unusual persons in charge of various activities, it will be stimulating to them to have an appreciative president. Furthermore, there will be many times during the year when the president will have to step into the breach. And, when key people drop out, replacements can be chosen with greater intelligence.

11

OFFICE MANAGEMENT

ONCE AGAIN WE ARE DISCUSSING A FIELD WHICH THEORETI-cally should not concern the president, and yet the office of a college is extremely important from two points of view. First, it means a great deal to students to be able to deal with a sympathetic and efficient office staff. Second, outsiders will get one of the fleeting but important impressions of the college from the office. You will find that it really operates as part of your guidance system. A great many so-called guidance questions are routine questions that can be and often are handled by office personnel. I have seen colleges where preactically the whole guidance was handled by the office secretary. Administrative officers were busy with "more important matters," instructors "didn't know anything about such matters," with the result that everything was dumped into her lap.

I believe firmly, as I state elsewhere in this book, that instructors and administrators should all know what is going on at the college, but I also feel that the office staff should be organized so that it can help students. I will agree that things should be so organized that each person and each office has its function. But I also know that students will not always go to the right person or the right office. When they start being shunted from one place to another, they just give up and don't bother to get their questions answered. The result is that unnecessary and serious errors occur. A student will get to the last semester and then realize that he still needs a year of something or other. Therefore, I say, let us give students as much mass guidance as possible, but let us also organize so that obvious answers can be given out quickly and easily by anyone on the teaching or office staffs. The body of catalogue knowledge isn't so great that any intelligent office secretary can't master it.

A word should be said about the physical appearance of offices. I believe that offices should be inviting, neat, and efficient looking. I remember one inspection committee I happened to serve on. Over a million dollars had been spent on the building we were inspecting, but the office had the most ill-assorted and run down furniture and equipment. It was depressing! And then I have been in offices where money has been spent to outfit them properly, but the personnel has allowed all sorts of things to accumulate, boxes of supplies, stacks of reports, files of papers, most of which should either be thrown away or stored neatly in closets or files. Institutions have a way of attracting clutter. A president should not give too many orders, but, periodically and alternately, two orders are necessary: Clear off all desks and tables, and clean out all files and closets. Leave only what is absolutely necessary; throw away what isn't needed, and use storage files for other materials.

One college president told me that when one of his teachers died, it took two days to clean out his office.

Recently, a friend of mine was appointed administrator of a professor's estate. She told me she used over 200 cartons to take away students' papers he had accumulated for the last thirty years. There is no reason why college offices, classrooms, or desks should become catch-alls for the trash that all of us accumulate. It costs a great deal of money to keep, let alone the space it usurps and the slovenly appearance it offers. I maintain that most instructors don't need more than one file drawer for current use. If a person is working on a special problem, then conceivably more might be needed. And so, the person in charge must know how to cope with this problem in a good-natured way.

Attention should be paid to the physical comfort of office personnel. Air conditioning in warm localities will pay dividends in happier and more efficient workers. Rest room facilities are important. Whenever possible, an attempt should be made to have the office staff feel that it is an important part of the college. We try to invite the office personnel to as many of the college functions and receptions as is physically possible. The office staff can serve as a sort of flywheel to correct the aberrations and erratic functioning of faculty in non-instructional matters.

Of course, every person has a different idea of how an office should operate. I think common sense can answer practically all of the questions that come up. My feeling is that the simpler it is, the better it is. And as far as possible let all of the offices be near each other. A small college doesn't have to be complicated. There is so much time wasted in inter-office memoranda! Things that should be accomplished simply and at the moment become the subject of complicated memos in quadruplicate taking weeks to flit back and forth. Keep things around the college simple so that the major attention can always be focused on good instruction and good guidance. Everything else is secondary!

The administrator is always faced with the problem of machines. This paragraph should be unnecessary and yet I have seen some institutions that buy almost every machine that is manufactured, and others with little more than a few old typewriters. There are a few things that can be said about machines. First, it is not a matter of how many machines you have, but how well they are taken care of, and how efficiently they are used. I have seen offices where good machines stood idle in corners and back rooms because no one was taking the trouble of having them serviced. Specific persons ought to be responsible for each machine. Do not let faculty and students use machines indiscriminately. If necessary, have special machines set apart for faculty and students, but even then someone has to watch over them. Have machines serviced regularly, whether typewriters, copying machines, addressing machines or postage meters. I recommend that you switch over to electric typewriters for your staff if you haven't already done so. I am in favor of mechanization within limits, perhaps because help is often hard to get. It is better to have one very good copying machine which functions efficiently than three or four indifferent ones in various stages of disrepair. The saving on important machines is nowhere as much as our friends, the glib salesmen, would have us believe, but it does make us less dependent on help. On the other hand, machines create problems also. When the machine breaks down, things are held up until the service man arrives. This is why properly trained staff members should operate the machines efficiently. One type of machine that is almost indispensable is the automatic typewriter that types each letter individually but fills in the salutation and other lines. It will pay dividends in fund raising, in public relations, even in every-day administration.

I believe that this should be true in a small college office especially. There ought to be prevalent such an *esprit de corps* that each person should be ready to help out the other person whenever the need arises. I would also make it clearly understood that such cooperation is expected, making sure, however, that we do not create conditions whereby slow or lazy persons have to be continually bailed out by the more efficient employees. Furthermore, every office person should be able to handle the switchboard, and all other machines so that in emergencies the widest possible flexibility is in order.

At this point, a college president has the right to say, "What do I know about all these things. I have my doctorate in English or science or philosophy and it was never my intention to be an office manager." True enough, and yet I believe it advisable for the administrator of a small institution to take a day now and then throughout the year to check on the office organization setup. And it will pay dividends, if for a few minutes each week he shows an interest in what goes on in the office, and expresses appreciation for work well done. There are so many ways in which office staff members can help a college in addition to their regular tasks. They will see things that don't occur to the academic mind.

Somewhat connected with office matters is the whole subject of printing, whether it be catalogue, promotional material, invitations or announcements. The president may have on his staff someone who has good taste and knows how to get good printing at reasonable cost. Usually he hasn't, and has to rely on the artistic quality of his printer. Again, the president had better learn the rudiments of good typographical forms. He won't have time to check on every printed piece that is issued from the institution, but at least he can convey some of his wishes to his subordinates and to the printers involved. Much of the time, good printing costs no more than the cheap, commercial kind. Watch styles of the larger institution which can afford to have editorial and typographical directors. I have found it worthwhile to keep a file of good typographical examples so that often I can denote color or type or get an idea of size. The same feeling for good styling ought to apply to students as well. They need direction too. Since cost is too often a factor, there is always the danger that the printer who doesn't know any better will foist upon them a cheap looking invitation or announcement. With all the attention in the world, there will be pieces that we shudder to look at. But it's also fun once in a while to help create an attractive form. As a matter of fact, I have often thought that somewhere in our required English or art courses there ought to be just a little bit about the preparation of acceptable printed matter. It is an art form, as far as I am concerned, equally as important as any other of our daily applications of good esthetic form, such as plateware or room layout or clothing.

12

CUSTODIAL SERVICE AND CONSTRUCTION

A SMALL COLLEGE MAY BE FORTUNATE ENOUGH TO HAVE A major domo in charge of custodial service who really knows what should be done and has it done properly. Some institutions are afflicted with a little dictator who does things his own way, and no young whippersnapper of a college president is going to tell him what to do. One public institution I know of has a well paid position in its budget, but the incumbent who got the position, because of veteran preference imposed by law, is too ill to work effectively. Probably every institution has a different arrangement and different expenses. All I can do in this chapter is to tell you what I should like to see in the custodial service and tell you frankly that few institutions are fortunate enough to have it.

I should like to have a person who knows what absolute cleanliness means, and who would have the institution spotless at all times. He would also be or have among his staff good handymen who would take care of all minor repairs. He would have his snow removal and his grass mowing machines always ready for action and used efficiently. His greatest asset would be that he would know how to get good workers, train them properly, and see that they produced a reasonable amount of work for every day's pay. This person must also be a genius at working with students. When the dances or the dramatic productions or the games come along, he will take care of the logistics of the situation and know how to utilize the students' energy, but always be ready to clean up when they don't follow through. He will know how to coordinate with the food service and whether it is a tea for a score or a dinner for five hundred, he will have tables and chairs moved, and make sure the red carpet is out for the guests. He will work efficiently with the administration whenever there are special functions or when commencement rolls around. Whenever it is necessary, he will work as many hours as the president does, and not complain that he could get only four hours sleep. He will get along with both students and faculty. He will realize that some members of both categories are naturally untidy, and that, gently but strictly, rules of neatness must be enforced.

Our friend, and he certainly would be our friend if he possessed all these qualities, will also be keenly conscious of all safety factors within the institution and will take proper precautions at all times. Fire equipment would be serviced regularly. He will have a loving care for all furniture and equipment. He will not simply fill the cellar with slightly broken furniture, but have it repaired within a reasonable period. He will work out regular schedules, especially during the summer and during Christmas and spring vacation periods, so that necessary painting and upkeep may be spaced efficiently through the year. And he will do all this on the modest salary a small institution can afford.

The use of student help can benefit most institutions.

I have found that students will be ready to do anything. It is advisable to have clear cut directions, and prompt checking of work. I believe a college has a moral obligation when it uses student help. Aside from the cost, if the college allows the student to give poor or inadequate work, it is encouraging the student in habits of laziness and dishonesty. The college should expect diligent and efficient service in return for reasonable pay.

But all of the above is day-to-day trivia, which theoretically should not take up any of the president's time, but which unfortunately will often jam up the day unmercifully. There is the larger problem of new buildings, additions, and construction of any kind.

A president should know something about architectural styles, about general contracting, and about construction in general. Whether it is the asphalt tiling of a room or the repair of a road, he will be drawn into the problem in some way. Let me give you an example of what I mean. When our college was very small we needed a faculty conference room. We decided to close in the veranda of our old castle. Bids from general contractors ran from $21,000 to $45,000, excluding furniture. By breaking up the job, we had it done for less than $8,000, including furniture. I have many general contractors among my friends, but I always tell them they have an occupational disease. They don't know how to add straight. The sum of all the parts comes out much, much larger than ordinary arithmetic books would indicate. Of course, there are reasons for the saving in the example I gave. First, small contractors with less overhead can work more cheaply. The boss himself is on the job and supervises while working himself. Let us not forget that the dean and I put in many hours supervising and directing, all of which was not figured in the cost. We bought our own lights at wholesale prices, and our own electricians put them in.

In my lifetime, I have gone through over fifty buildings, large and small. You will find, as I have, that the spread between the lowest and the highest bid is most often enormous. I used to have bids opened before the entire student body. I would invite the bidders and the architect to sit on the stage. The president of the student body would open the bids; the secretary would write them on a blackboard. It was a good experience for the students and they had a part in the building of the college. I would have a set of the architect's specifications and the blueprints on a table in the library and many students would look at them, especially engineering and business majors. Three times during the building process, I or the contractor would take students through the unfinished building and point out the various stages of construction.

At the opening of the bids, I would have the students ask questions. One usual question was "What guarantee is there that the contractor will finish the job?" The architect would then explain that a performance bond was required. I would then ask the students what decision they would recommend. In one case, a library, the students recommended that the trustees not take the lowest bid but the next higher bid which was $10,000. more but the builder had stated he would build it in six months less time. The students reasoned that it was worth $10,000. to have the library a semester earlier. And the trustees adopted the recommendation.

Certain members of the administration and of the faculty have found that by taking a little time off, studying problems and costs, we have saved sizeable sums. Out of 3,000 institutions in America, a few hundred may have unlimited funds for construction. We were in the vast majority that didn't, and we had to make every dollar count. In a small institution, you have to know something about construction, otherwise you become the victim of glib sales talk. Common sense and good taste will usually solve many of the problems that come along. You'll make mistakes, but so will architects, contractors, estimators and experts. At least you'll have the fun of making your own mistakes and not paying for the faulty thinking of someone else. No commercial representative, not even the architect, can know the needs of the institution and the use of rooms and equipment as well as you do yourself.

13

THE LIBRARY

FOR THE SMALL COLLEGE, THE LIBRARY IS OFTEN A MAJOR problem. I have seen libraries in institutions of several hundred that were no more than a paltry collection of cast-off books and free magazines. On the other hand, I have seen some libraries of small institutions that would have done credit to universities. Every college president wants to have his library housed in a separate building. We seem to make a fetish of the number of buildings we have. As a matter of fact, it makes just as much sense to have a library inside a main building as it does to have it housed separately. The only disadvantage I see is that usually in such a building there is lack of stack space. And, of course, we have to have a lot of stack space to store the thousands of volumes no one reads anymore. And, we must not dispose of them away because we could not keep up the ever-increasing grand total of volumes in the library!

I maintain that a small college has no right to try to compete with a university library. The functions of the two types are basically different in that the university has to provide for graduate research. I think it would make sense to say that for a small institution, once it has built up a certain number of volumes considered appropriate for its size, to dispose of old volumes and resist further temptations to boast of larger totals. It will grow slowly even then, but it will be a sounder library. I can hear some librarians saying "That's what you're supposed to do anyway." My only answer is that it usually isn't done that way.

It would seem to me that the college library should have three major functions. The first would be the traditional one of being an adjunct to the classroom. The second, which I consider almost as important is to encourage informal and independent reading by the student. The third is to help in the professional and personal development of the teacher. It would seem to me almost basic to have freshmen given an orientation course in the use of the library, and yet in how many cases is this not done thoroughly or at all? It is my definite impression that the larger the institution, the more likely the mechanics of the arrangements will defeat the best of plans. The second step is the concept of library use that should pervade the whole faculty. Common sense has to play a part in all educational plans and particularly so in library matters. It is ridiculous to expect the mathematics instructor to have as high an incidence of library use as the English or social science instructor. I have seen cases in physics and mathematics, to give two examples, where instead of concentrating on the orderly use of a perfectly good class text, the students were regimented into the library to pick out things here and there, and finally come out with a confused picture that did not contribute to educational growth.

I believe also that in too many cases the emphasis on excerpts and multiplicity of references leads to hodge podge impressions that do a disservice to students. The use of the library can not be neatly summarized into regulations. Assignments must be based on common sense and will differ from classroom to classroom. There are two important things to watch. The first is enthusiastic motivation and the second is a good system of checking by the instructor.

It seems to me that today the library is a different place than it was fifty years ago. At that time, the emphasis was on books. Today, pamphlets, special reports, daily papers, special magazines will often be more important references than books which are old almost by the time they are off the press. Two generations ago, there was, relatively speaking, a small number of books that formed the common heritage and that most people referred to. Today, many of these books still form important source materials. But, in addition, since the tempo of life has accelerated, we have all these other materials. Added to all of this is an increasing disinclination on the part of people, old and young, to read because of competing and distracting activities. The colleges really have a problem on their hands. One might say that while it is necessary for the college student to read more and more, he finds less and less time to read. I would say that it is the most important institutional problem today and one that must be solved continually and jointly by the members of the teaching and staffs. It is my strong belief that the small college is in a better position to do a better job than the larger institutions.

In the small college, the library staff can communicate more easily and can keep abreast of what the teaching staff is trying to do. It is probably easier to have a silent study period for a class directed jointly by the instructor and the librarian. There is the possibility that the librarian may be able to suggest to the instructor new references. Finally, there is the possibility of getting new books or materials quickly without the usual bureaucratic system that operates in large institutions.

But when we have tried every device possible to make the library an adjunct of the classroom, we should still hope to encourage the young people to use the library for leisure and personal reading. To me, that is the greatest test of the effectiveness of a library. If the librarian can entice students to have an interest in books and to take them out informally for pleasurable voluntary reading, then he has achieved the ultimate. Perhaps we should use some of the merchandising methods of commercial book shops.

Publishers spend so much money to make attractive jackets! Why throw them out. Let's use them to attract readers. And let's put these gaily covered books so that they practically hit the students in the face. Let's use every trick of the trade! Some students may even read the abridged one volume Gibbons if it's tied up with the latest movie. When *Moulin Rouge* hit the local theaters, we trotted out all the beautiful books on French painting. Books on jobs, hobbies, athletics, fashion will always draw readers.

It may be objected that these books are not in the realm of college reading. I would say that we are faced with two problems: first to get students to read more regardless of quality, second, to raise their sights on the type of books. I am going to make an assertion that I am sure many people will disagree with. I don't think men college graduates read very much once they graduate. The women do read a book once in a while. A buyer for one of the large chains of bookstores told me he bought books in the proportion of ten to one favoring women and I believe that it is so. I believe I saw some statistics that the average high school graduate has not read five books through and completely in his lifetime. I shudder to think what the statistics would be for the American colleges.

I believe that college students should read some books completely. Granted, some books need not be read except for excerpts or certain chapters. But the student should have as many experiences as possible of reading books through as quickly as possible—giving uninterrupted attention to the book at least an hour or two at a time. It makes me feel dejected when I see a professional man who presumably represents the highest cultural group take two or three months to read a relatively short book. And then when he has finished it, he feels he has achieved intellectual heights!

All of this is tied up with reading and I can't see how we can talk about library objectives if students haven't attained certain skills in reading. Colleges have a three-cornered problem: class instruction, reading, library. To argue that students should have good reading habits before they enter college is beside the point. Many of them won't and strangely enough many students in the top quartile won't. Success in college depends to a large extent on reading. For the library to be effective, students must know how to read well—to read for comprehension and to read speedily.

The matter of open or closed stacks always comes up for discussion. Here again, the small college has an advantage in that it can have open stacks. The large institution usually can not. Open stacks have a disadvantage, of course. Books disappear. I maintain it is worth the extra expense. Usually the losses are much smaller than we suppose, and strangely enough are more than made up by the saving of expense on extra personnel. The important point is that the more interesting books are made, the more chance that students will read them.

A word should be said about service for faculty members. The library should seek to provide professional, cultural, and general reading books for the staff. Faculty members need encouragement too and an institution will gain far more than the cost by providing as much reading material as possible for its teaching staff. It does not mean that the person studying for his doctorate should expect to have placed in the library all the specialized tomes bearing on his problem. The university library where he is getting his doctorate should make these books available. However, here and there, the college library, through the inter-university exchange which operates in most states and throughout the country, may be able to help in the case of individual volumes.

I believe college libraries should give major thought to their microfilm department. I am simply thrilled with the possibilities of microfilm—for a number of reasons. First is the saving of space. Second is the fact that we can get volumes which otherwise would be unobtainable or prohibitive in cost. Third is my feeling that in some cases students will be encouraged to do more effective work by reading a large screen. Proper accommodation should be made for a bank of microfilm projectors and students and faculty should be given adequate guidance in their use. Furthermore, in the library budget, rational emphasis should be placed on increasing the store of the microfilm collection.

One of my faculty who was a Rhodes scholar tells me of the awful days he spent in some of the old libraries. The students were wrapped in old gowns to protect them from the cold. Each one would sit almost motionless before his tome. There would be an occasional wiping of a most nose and once in a while a very subdued nod to a fellow scholar. Needless to say, those days are gone forever for our students. Except for a small number of bookish individuals, our students are riproaring hell bent for excitement and the last thing they want to do is to sit quietly in a library for long periods and pore over books. It will take every bit of motivation, regulation, and pleasurable persuasion to achieve the reading they should do as college students. And in all of this, we are aiming not merely for the mechanical accomplishment of the daily or the weekly assignment but the acquiring of lifelong habits of leisure and professional reading.

One aspect most often forgotten is the archival collection. While I was writing *A History of Higher Education in New Jersey*, I found that only three of the sixty institutions within the state had such a collection. And yet, this should be part of the library: histories or theses written regarding the college, articles on the college, newspaper clippings, photographs, books by the faculty, catalogues, yearbooks, student newspapers and magazines, programs of functions including commencements. When I retired, one of the things I did to keep myself busy was to start the Fairleigh Dickinson University Archival Collection. To date there are fourteen volumes which include copies of speeches, memoranda to the trustees and to the faculty, important experimental projects, remembrances of the early days by the faculty and by alumni, and important historical aspects. As part of the archives, although it is stored in the visual aids department, are motion picture shorts of important talks given at the university. A college should keep a record of its history. These archival volumes are not printed. Only fifteen copies are xeroxed and then bound. They are placed in the various libraries of our own university and in other key research libraries. To give you three quick examples of the sort of material included in these volumes: the facsimile of the bill of sale of the original castle where our college started, the document that legalized the change of name, the yearly survey we made of high school graduates, all items that are lost in the shuffle of files.

Another aspect of the library that should be shown to all students is the reference book area. Of course, some students become involved with it in certain courses, but I maintain that all students ought to be familiar with most of its tomes. To give you three examples: inevitably in most peoples' lives, it is important to have a list of newspapers in an area. How many people are familiar with *Ayer's Directory of Newspapers?* A list of companies in the state and facts regarding them—all in the Industrial Index. A list of legislators—how few realize most states have a state directory. The emphasis is, of course, on literary and historical references, but our lives, if in anyway productive, are bound to be involved with many other diverse reference needs. I have seen students build life careers on each one of the reference volumes cited above.

Lastly, I feel strongly that the college should encourage students to acquire books, not only with texts studied in class, but also a library of interesting books for personal enjoyment. The college library ought to share some of the aspects of an interesting and well stocked bookstore. One redeeming feature on most campuses is that many college bookstores are, in a way, supplementing the role of the library. Those of you who have visited the fourth floor library of the University Club in New York will undoubtedly have been fascinated by the many volumes not in stacks but on tables to lure the passerby. I feel all libraries ought to have the same attractive displays. It doesn't fit in with neat library techniques and undoubtedly it may encourage pilfering but, nevertheless, it is bound to encourage reading and that's what libraries are for.

14

SMALL COLLEGES CAN SURVIVE

A SMALL COLLEGE STILL HAS A CHANCE TO SURVIVE IN SPITE of the competition in higher education. But it has to limit its scope of activities and seek excellence within that scope. It has been my observation that as an institution becomes larger, its expenses increase geometrically. I know this sounds wrong if we think of large scale manufacturing, but I feel certain that any studies would show this disproportionate increase to be true in most cases. We are talking, of course, of the small, private college of limited resources and, for the sake of this discussion, let us think in terms of 2,000 students, although it is difficult to draw the line at any particular point.

The small college can exist provided its resources are used wisely and not wasted. Let it not look to the large public colleges, nor to the rich private colleges nor to private urban universities for guidance. The first two have the money for their needs in spite of their wailings to the contrary. The third have serious problems of their own.

Yet, the small private college has certain advantages. But let us first enumerate the things it can not do.

1. It can not support a doctoral-level graduate school on the shoulders of the undergraduate. I realize the faculty will wage a continuing pressure to provide upward organization but the lines have to be drawn somewhere, and if the understanding on this limitation is clear, there is less opportunity for squabbling on this issue. However, assuming that the faculty has the proper professional training, there is no reason why masters' programs cannot be combined with the upper two years to form a three-year sequence.

2. It can not seek to solve community and broad social problems that cost money and that would, in effect, be paid for indirectly by the undergraduate. If the community or the state or the federal government wants a special problem solved, then it should pay for it, and not just simply the out-of-pocket cost but whatever the true proportionate cost will be. There is no reason why the state should pour hundreds of millions into tax-supported universities and then expect private institutions of limited means to rush in and solve problems simply because its easier on the state budget.

3. It can not support an athletic superstructure or even a top-heavy physical training program. All this costs money and the undergraduate has to pay for it, one way or another.

4. It can not support a top-heavy administrative staff. I know it is popular with accrediting committees to suggest all types of supportive personnel. They don't have to pay the bill. Too many private institutions have overreached themselves in the creation of new administrative

positions, with the result that the emphasis is on empire-building, the issuance of padded reports that no one reads, the multiplicity of vacuous, time-wasting conferences that add nothing to the service to the student, and the issuance of thousands of memos and counter-memos that create an air of dispiriting confusion.

5. It can not support an expensive research program. Whatever research takes place must be done by faculty members on their own or must be supported by outside grants. And it is important to make sure these temporary grants do not create permanent empires.

6. It can not support a superabundance of low enrollment elective courses.

Let the emphasis be on the student and the faculty, and this does not mean that either has to run away with the institution. It does mean that everything that is done is intended to serve the student better. It does mean that expenses of all types are watched carefully so that the main thrust is on faculty remuneration. Does this mean that the small private college can pay salaries competitive with rich universities that have doctoral programs and with large tax-supported institutions? It can not and any attempt to do so can only lead to eventual disaster.

The private college had a *raison d'être* as long as states supported public institutions niggardly or almost not at all. But today most states are generously supporting state universities, state colleges, and community colleges. One can observe what is happening by noting that the number of new private colleges is practically nil and, conversely, each year a number of private colleges close their doors. At this point in history there are three alternatives for a small private institution: to close, to be

taken over by the state or by a more efficient or wealth-
ier private university, or to operate efficiently within its
limits. To close is unthinkable for the great majority.
The state can not possibly take them all over, especially
since in many states the saturation point has been
reached as far as expenses for public higher education.
Very few private universities are operating efficiently
enough or have enough funds to take on additional
burdens. I maintain that it is possible for the third alternative to operate.

The advantage of this cohesiveness, I suggest, should
mean good service for the students. I am old fashioned
enough to expect that all faculty members should demand extensive reading, high standards in frequent
writing assignments, and rational discussion at all times
in all classes. Let us not have a lecturing college, but
when lectures do take place they should be well prepared and delivered effectively. Yes, I believe in disciplined approaches to learning.

But I also believe that the traditional five subject
yearly program should be reduced to four and that we
should give the student the right, but not the obligation, to take a fifth subject on an independent basis
either through cassettes or through some other means
of self-study. There are thousands of such courses available and the library should make them available. I
would give faculty members the opportunity to make
up their own special course on cassettes, so that a student could study at his convenience, consult with the
professor from time to time, and upon finishing the
course ask for an examination. There should be a very
modest fee of $200 paid by the university to the faculty
member for his service. It's a good source of extra income for the professor, somewhat like writing a textbook, but more important, it could give him income and

a modicum of activity after retirement. I would allow those students who seem to be mature enough to pursue independent research or an out-of-class educative experience to substitute this for one of the four required courses. I would encourage this but I would make sure that this phase would come under the strict supervision of faculty members who would require periodic reports, related readings and a final report and/or examination.

While the faculty of such a college would not be expected to produce the dazzling research of larger, richer institutions higher up in doctoral echelons, (although I suspect that there will be just as much, proportionately, as in most universities), I would expect that faculty members be widely read in their own fields and have wide cultural interests outside their field. But it is important that the campus have a well-integrated cultural ambiance involving the theater, music, art and special lectures. Let the administration, faculty and students work this program out together. (I wish I could say that students by themselves could work out an ideal program. The probability is that one would wind up with a succession of rock-and-roll artists all hired at inflated prices.) It would serve to set cultural standards even though there may be grousing. Incidentally we should encourage the faculty to come out to all the affairs. Let the college community enjoy a mature, diversified program that combines socializing and cultural uplift. It has to be an all-embracing, cooperative, zestful undertaking. This is the sort of thing that doesn't happen in a large cafeteria-type, impersonal university.

If the college is in a region where evening sessions are a possibility, it is in luck. The evening session can help to share in the support of the library, the laboratories, the maintenance of the buildings, and promotion. The use of the campus during the summer and the holding of special summer institutes are other possibilities not only to keep the college in the black but to give the faculty members added opportunities to supplement their income. If faculty members are going to moonlight—and increasing members are doing so—it is better for them to do so on their own campuses. Let's do away with hypocrisy.

Young people, in spite of their rebellious and independent spirit, react to guidance, to rational, disciplined programs with possibilities for free-wheeling activities, and to a friendly intellectual ambiance where the love of one's fellow being is a dominant principle. Don't be thrown off by two or three loud mouthed students who enjoy the power of being rabble rousers. Sometimes one of these may succeed in becoming the student newspaper editor or president of the student council. Consult with the whole student council on problems but also call in from time to time non-office-holding students. They have good minds too and what they say may be just as representative as elected student officers. I would not forget the directors of guidance of the high schools in the region. While, presumably, many colleges will seek to draw students from as wide a region as possible, the greatest possibilities exist within a 100-mile radius. If these guidance directors are impressed with the sincerity of the college's operation, with the excellence of its programs, and with the conscientiousness of the faculty, they will send a certain proportion of their students to the college.

The very fact that the institution is small should give it a great educational advantage. Every student will know most of the other students and the faculty will know most of the students well.

But in a small college, if there is vibrant leadership with high professional standards, there is apt to be a minimum of peccadillos of young teachers such as teaching without adequate preparation, not maintaining class or office schedules, indifferent grading or reading assignments, slipshod attention to meetings or routine matters. Old fashioned? Perhaps. But in my experience I have observed that the real professional leaders, the real workers, are very meticulous in their observance of classroom schedules and routine necessities.

I feel strongly that a private college ought to operate on the principle of fifty per cent income (tuition plus endowment income) for faculty and administrative salaries, twenty five per cent for non-teaching expenses and the rest for capital expenses and additions to the endowment fund. The trustees should agree to this principle and the faculty should understand it.

Usually I get opposition from those who have never had to operate a college, and whose experience has been with rich or tax-supported institutions. You can tamper with this formula for a few years but eventually the verities of life will catch up with you.

In this onward rush for bigness, for buildings, for administrative complexity, we have drifted away from concern with quality of life. The small college does have the opportunity to recapture this spirit.

Having said this about small college operation, I feel the same thing applies to small units or colleges within larger institutions. It was this compelling idea that led me to set up an experimental college, Edward Williams College, within the framework of a large university. The educational leader of a unit, be it 400 or 600 or 1200 in size, has an opportunity to have higher standards of service to students that obtain in an impersonal over-organized mammoth institution.

15

COLLECTIVE BARGAINING

THREE YEARS, AGO, AS I STARTED TO WRITE ANOTHER BOOK *Demanage Higher Education,* I knew less about collective bargaining than about any other phase, since I had never been involved with unions during my presidency. I decided to learn as much about the subject as I could and kept careful track of the time involved. I spent three days in Washington talking to union officials; I spoke to the local National Labor Relations Board administrators; I spoke to college presidents, to faculty bargaining representatives, to management representatives, and of course I read a great deal. I read books, important articles, government brochures, union leaflets; but above all I read twenty one college and university bargaining contracts now in existence.

How long did it take me to know as much as I felt I needed to know? Two weeks. I mention this because most persons who assume a college presidency or who may be thrown into the position of representing management in collective bargaining will have to learn, and learn quickly everything there is to know about the subject. But it isn't that difficult. And there is only one way to know, and that is to plunge into the subject and immerse one's self in it until one is knowledgeable about it.

What are the reasons that faculty members seek to unionize? Occasionally, it may be because of a strong philosophic belief in unionism. Or it may be resentment of an authoritarian president, or a reaction to a weak one who, they feel, will lead the institution downhill; or they may not have confidence in the board of trustees. Most often there is an economic fear, fear of not getting good salaries, fear for job security or even a whole unit being abolished, fear of being discharged or not promoted.

Perhaps faculty members may have observed that unions have upgraded salaries in other institutions and hope that the same thing will happen in their case.

Union activity has been greatest in certain states: New York (about ⅙ of eligible institutions have chosen to unionize), New Jersey, Illinois, Michigan, California. Proximity to a union office means that it is easier for the organizers to reach a certain college or university. Or sometimes the institution has a small clique of dedicated union activists. Sometimes unionization takes place because it seems to be a fad to do so and faculty members may feel they are missing out on something. Lastly, the fact that there are three national unions: the American Federation of Teachers, the American Association of University Professors, and the National Education Association, has produced a curious result in some institutions. Instead of the issue being union or no union, the issue becomes instead, shall it be the A.A.U.P., the A.F.T. or the N.E.A.? When this happens, it seems that the votes usually are very close. The fundamental issue is obscured and in the heat of discussion as to which union is best, the alternative of no union is forgotten. In some states, a two-step process is required: first, on the issue of unionizing, second, which union. Now there is talk of the A.A.U.P. merging with one of the other unions.

The Yeshiva decision has thrown the unionization movement into disarray. Since faculty is involved in what are essentially managerial decisions, the institution does not need to embrace a union legally. Things are at a standstill. Other colleges which could follow the example of Yeshiva have hesitated to do so. The unions apparently are not forcing the issue, at least not for the time being. But other factors are operating too. The economic squeeze in most states has led to the dropping of thousands of positions and the unions are powerless to prevent this. As far as I can observe, strikes where they have occurred, while they have been unpleasant for the administration, have usually not solved anything although here and there they may have cowed the president or the board to accede to the union's demands.

The pattern that has evolved in the United States has really risen from the union movement in the public elementary and high schools. Then the two-year public colleges along with a few four-year public and independent colleges have taken up the cause and, all of a sudden, spurred especially by public institutions, the movement has spread mostly to large colleges and universities. I suspect that smaller colleges tend to remain out of the movement because there aren't enough union dues generated to make up for the expensive costs of launching a unit. But the rivalry between the unions may wind up by being a disservice to the institution and to the faculty. Usually, thirty per cent of the faculty must request an election for a bargaining unit.

What should the administrator do when the issue of unionization reaches a campus? This is an issue that must be tackled head-on by the trustees and the president. Two alternatives are open. One is to acquiesce and to let the faculty make its own decision. The other is to take a stand and to make that stand and the reasons for it known to the faculty. At any rate, there should be open debate on the subject. At this point it will be almost necessary to arrange for the services of a labor lawyer who can advise on which steps are legal and which are not. The trustees should choose two of their number to work with the president. Both the trustees and the president, if they haven't done so already, should plunge into a cram course on faculty collective bargaining, much as I did, and start off by reading three good books on the subject and about twenty collective bargaining contracts, and have a series of questions-and-answer periods with the labor lawyer, who should be a person with hard negotiating experience. There is no point in getting upset about the turn of events or becoming emotional about it. It is best to pursue an objective course, clinically, efficiently, quietly.

Above all, management must listen carefully and attentively to the faculty. Let's face it, the old collegial spirit is gone. Now administrators are management and faculty are employees. The faculty is going to make the decision for the institution. And trustees, administrators, or faculty members who think that unionization and collegiality can be mixed in the union are being very naive indeed. A word of caution: it is useless to make concessions to ward off a union. It simply makes it that much harder when one gets into bargaining.

Looking at the movement from the outside, I personally feel that it would be better not to have collective bargaining. The greatest move forward in faculty salaries was made when the A.A.U.P., then not a union, began to rate colleges and universities. Three other factors have played a part: the shortage of college teachers at a time of great increases in enrollment, the Ford Foundation grants for faculty increases, and the pressure exerted by accrediting associations, especially in the realm of fringe benefits. It is beginning to be evident now that, as far as four-year colleges are concerned, there is very little difference, if at all, between unionized and non-unionized institutions as far as salary and fringe benefits are concerned. And unions have had a minimal effect on retrenchment when it becomes necessary because of economic factors.

There is no question in my mind that the creation of an adversary spirit is very unfortunate. The concept of creating a procrustean bed so that a college organization can be fitted into an industrial labor mold is wrong. This does not mean that a standing faculty committee should not present suggestions for salary schedules and fringe benefits. The days when faculty were expected to work for genteel wages are over. They were over from the early fifties as higher education became sophisticated in such matters. Now it all boils down to how much money is available, public or private.

But once the decision is made on unionization, the broad question to be decided is whether governance is to be included in collective bargaining. I believe that from both the faculty and the administrative points of view, it is wrong to include it. Let the union limit itself to salary and fringe benefits. Governance matters can best be handled in faculty senates. Thus colleges can retain some vestiges of a profession. It is in this area that there is the greatest lack of expertise, of clear thinking, of naiveté.

That first contract is going to be the most important

and the most basic. There should be a cut-off date for submitting faculty demands. Then there should be a reasonable period for management to analyze the demands. This period is apt to be much longer than future waiting periods. It should be stated at this point that it is important to know which subjects are mandatory and which are voluntary or permissive. It should be remembered that boards of trustees retain their rights by federal or state laws and by their charter. The agenda for a future meeting should be agreed upon so that both sides may do their proper preparation. It is better for management to tackle non-economic matters first and thus retain their leverage on economic issues. Unions have had the most sophisticated and the most experienced consultants available. Administrative staffs and trustees have been caught unprepared. As a result there has been a great deal of muddled thinking and arrangement, and what I would describe as administrative clumsiness. It should be noted that some labor negotiators feel themselves that unionization and collegiality are mutually exclusive. Some administrators try to be overly anxious to please the faculty negotiators, and this, so far as seasoned and knowledgeable labor and management negotiators are concerned, is fallacious.

The trustees have to choose the management negotiators. The trustees and the president should stay out but be continuously informed of developments. I believe that in time colleges and universities, especially the larger ones, will have to have an administrator whose main job will be in collective bargaining. This is an example of how the process costs money, money which could better be used for other purposes. What are some of the dangers in having an administrator who already has other duties on this team? The pressure of other activities may not leave him enough time for collective bargaining. He becomes physically tired out. Also his heart may not be in it and he has a feeling that he wants to bend over backwards to be fair to the faculty. Perhaps he isn't tough enough to stand the pressures of the opposing team. He may cringe at unfavorable newspaper publicity. He hates to have the faculty against him. It could even be that he secretly hopes that the faculty will get a big raise so that it will bump upwards his own salary.

Let's face it, collective bargaining is a hard process. The management negotiator has to be able to anticipate demands. He can't be a passive, timid, ineffectual partner in the bargaining room. Incidentally, too many deliberations are needlessly protracted. There are some minor items, especially if they come at the tail end, that can be submitted to outside arbitration. Usually, trade-offs at the end are inevitable.

Where do the students stand in all this? In the past there has been a tendency for students to push for the faculty, but as I see it, this is diminishing for two reasons: professional salaries are not as comparatively low as they were, and students realize that any increases will be reflected in increased tuition, and this is so whether in private or public institutions. Faculty members do not have the right to stir up students, but they often do so because they have a natural opportunity to do so. Where this happens, it seems to me that management should have the right to publicize the faculty salaries plus the extent of fringe benefits plus summer, overtime and now intersession teaching. In other words, management should have an equal opportunity to present its case.

What is happening in most institutions, whether public or private, is that less money is available. The few very wealthy institutions which are, in the main, not involved with unionism anyway, are not doing badly. But most private institutions are faced with diminishing enrollments; most public institutions are faced with more restrictive budgets. Unions by themselves can not create money. They can only exert pressure as to how it may be allocated.

When the time comes that expenditures have to be curtailed, what takes place? First a certain unit within the institution may have to be cut out and in spite of pious resistance and cosmetic statements by the rest of the faculty not affected, there will be a quick adjustment to the dropping of the unit, once it happens. Second, cuts will be suggested by the faculty in everything else: maintenance, non-teaching expenses, administrative, student services. Third, if positions have to be dropped it will be the non-tenured positions at the lower schedules. Lastly, there will be a last ditch struggle to keep up, at least, the regular increments in salary. This is the unfortunate aspect of diminished available resources, and with the tightening tax situation and the effects of the lower birth rate, there are apt to be recurring instances of such diminutions.

The concept of tenure which was really started by Dr. Henry Wriston, formerly president of Brown University, was intended to prevent the ousting of a professor because of differing religious concepts. It was basically a concept of academic freedom. By extension, it has come to mean the right to occupy a position as long as that position is open. But now it has been twisted into "guaranteed employment" or "guaranteed annual wage," and this no institution can do unless it wants to set up a fantastically expensive insurance system that would cover possibilities of any number of positions being dropped.

The use of arbitration is a new dimension in higher education disputes, and while judicious use has to be made of it when both parties are near the end of an agreement, loose ends can be left to arbitrators so that the general agreement can be signed and a tense situation brought to an end.

Can you leave all of the collective bargaining to arbitration? I don't think so. Arbitrators tend to compromise. Management states it can give only three per cent; employees want seven per cent. Arbitrators may quickly give five per cent. But it isn't as easy as that, and perhaps the three percent is all the institution *can* give. I believe the real costly issues, the heavy issues, have to be worked out by the two opposing forces.

One of the questions often in dispute is whether chairmen should be considered "employees" or "management." The union point of view generally is that if he is to teach, if he is elected by the faculty, and if he does not have authority to hire and fire, then he should be unionized. If on the other hand he is appointed by the administration, then he is a member of the management team. Since the appointment of a chairman differs in different institutions, there is no clear-cut general rule to follow. This is one of those areas which makes unionization in higher education different from industrial unionization. At the present time some chairmen are unionized; some are not. But one thing is certain: There is bound to be an increase in the non-unionized "assistant deans" who will carry out "management" roles.

Now, observe what is happening as far as the hallowed position of the board of trustees is concerned. It is no longer a free agent or a court of final authority. Now it is hemmed in by national and state laws, by the rulings of Labor Relations Boards and official arbitrators, and by court decisions. The president and trustee, backed by a knowledgeable labor lawyer, have to know as much as possible about union operations in order to avoid having unions acquiring power by default. The more union activity there is, the greater need there is for truly educational leadership by the president, otherwise the institution is engulfed in a totality of grievances, fancied or real, in continuous bickering almost to the exclusion of fundamental purposes of education. And throughout, the administrator has to be fortified by maximum knowledge, a sense of balance and above all, humility. It boils down to a feeling of sincerity that the president and the board must have. A faculty has the basic right to unionize and this right must be respected even though the governing body may deplore it.

16

THE LAST FEW DECADES

EVERY SO OFTEN OVER THE CENTURIES CERTAIN DISCERNIBLE developments take place in higher education. As we have seen, after World War II America committed itself to some form of post-secondary education for all adults and, aided by loosening of purse strings by state legislatures and federal funding, there occurred a spurt that was probably greater than anything that had happened since the beginning of the century. What were some of the concomitants of this unprecedented expansion?

Too many institutions became too large for rational management. We had traditionally been thinking of a college as a small place, a few hundred or even a thousand or two, where there was maximum communication among the administration, faculty and students. Now, in a relatively short period, a sense of anonymity pervaded most campuses with almost a complete breakdown in communication between students and the institution. The number of administrators proliferated beyond reason. All sorts of new empires were born almost overnight. Each office was busy sending memoranda to all other offices and an intricate and expensive layer of new services was added to the basic function of learning.

Until the Second World War, it might be said that teachers in general had been subsidizing higher education by accepting genteel salaries so that tuition could be kept low. But now, during the last two decades, faculty members insisted on receiving renumeration commensurate with their work, and in increasing numbers even resorted to some form of bargaining arrangement with the institutions.

Over the same two decades, tuition in private institutions increased tenfold. It is difficult to pin down the exact increase in the cost of public higher education but probably if we limit the analysis to the cost of taking care of full-time students, and include in the expenses monies allocated to other funds, such as pensions, interest, amortization of capital expenses, and special grants, the increase would probably be about the same percentage as the rise in tuition in private institutions.

This has been a period when moonlighting as a substitute for scholarly research became a respectable activity, especially in large or urban institutions. But sometimes the moonlighting was not overt and often there was the temptation to engage in teaching in other institutions or to set up a business of one's own or to hire out as a business consultant. The danger here is that the professor, being secure in tenure in his university position, may tend to put his most creative effort into the other activity. In the whole turmoil of complicated campus activity, the old concept of the professor being on campus most of the week ready to speak to students at almost any time of the day has faded out of the picture. It may still exist in some small colleges, but it is an increasing rarity. In too many cases, the institution winds up with a full-time faculty member really teaching part time.

This has been the age when the number of committees grew to unmanageable proportions. Simple decisions that might have taken five minutes of administrative time now become matters of lengthy deliberations stretching over months. Everything had to be discussed ad nauseam. Excessive committee work tends to discourage innovative and creative work by faculty members and forces them to devote their major attention to trivia and wasteful details. Now a professor has three choices open to him after teaching his classes: scholarly work, moonlighting, or committee meetings.

This has been an age when more and more was spent on teaching and electronic hardware than probably in the whole life of higher education since colonial times, without any appreciable educational results except possibly in isolated instances. Most of this equipment was paid for by foundation and government grants in a varliant effort to encourage schools to become more efficient. To be sure, while the grants endured, the published results seemed to bear fruit. But mechanical gadgetry has left the main bulk of the teaching profession cold. Here and there, in new colleges, mostly in new two-year institutions, some thrilling experiments with cassette instruction may indicate the wave of the future but the real test will come when the present faculty of new institutions will have acquired tenure and may revert to the traditional lecture method. *"Plus ça change, plus c'est la même chose"*—that trite saying is nowhere truer than it is in higher education.

This has been the age when students began to insist that their point of view should enter into administrative and educational decisions. To be sure, progressive administrators since the earliest times have always involved students. But now students were rebelling against irrelevant education, against rigid curricular structures, against all forms of discipline.

This has been an age when more grandiose buildings were erected within a thirty-year period than had been erected since the turn of the century. The 1963 Education Act, massive bond issues, multimillionaire alumni who had to find some way of perpetuating their names, all collaborated to create an era of building that would have done Rome proud. College presidents and architects cooperated gleefully to add luster to their own professional reputations. How did this affect the students? Most couldn't be less impressed, and for a very simple reason: they had already been used to sparkling, new buildings in their high schools, many of which would make good college campuses. On the one hand, the institutions were spending billions to create the most magnificent buildings in history, and on the other students were developing the sloppiest era known since the days of François Villon in Paris. Glistening buildings on the outside; instant decay inside. The truth is that you don't need fancy buildings to achieve good education. The best classroom in the world is no classroom and in a sense the students have a point. "Look," they say, "we don't need luxury, we need love."

But rigid curricular requirements are breaking down and students are learning how to make end runs in qualifying for degrees. In the complexity of things, one little requirement is dropped and presto, a department finds that it no longer enjoys the captive students it formerly had. Examinations without attendance can wipe out a lot of classes. Other unexpected things are happening too.

Expensive and hastily built dormitories have a high

rate of vacancies. In their new search for freedom, while coeducational dormitories are nice, one's own little pad has a greater sense of intimacy. Besides, three or four people (or a couple of couples), setting up a cooperative apartment can come out better financially now that dormitories are getting more and more expensive.

Since time immemorial, students have turned thumbs down on institutional food in spite of valiant efforts to please them. They still feel that a hamburger cooked in their own lodging is better than a regular meal under the house plan. A few of them do turn out meals that would do honor to mother; a few others, adherents of natural or organic food, do manage to have a more nutritional regimen. But the rest, probably the great majority, get into the worst possible habits of pizza or fried fish and chips at odd times or when the spirit moves them.

The greatest wastage is of space. The effort to provide all sorts of facilities for students in too many cases has resulted in a great deal of unused space. In one institution, every time a student sits down in a chair, there are fourteen other unused spaces, not only in other classrooms but in libraries, athletic facilities, social rooms, he could be occupying. All of this has to be paid for either by students through tuition, or by taxpayers or by wealthy donors, and all three are becoming disenchanted with the way money is being used.

I think that the day of the small college, intelligently, creatively, and efficiently administered, may be due for a comeback, whether we think of an independent small college or one forming a part of a larger complex.

It is my experience that as a college becomes larger, expenses increase at a faster rate than tuition income. A small college may have a deficit but it will be a manageable one. It can recapture some of the things we have lost in the education explosion—a concern for the individual, sense of professional dignity, the opportunity to witness intellectual growth whether in the students or faculty. Neither size, nor monumental buildings, nor gadgetry, nor befuddling pseudo-democracy serve the human being.

Bigness is the curse of everything in this world, whether it is in business, in government, or in education. I think therefore that the college units, no bigger than 2,000, have the same opportunity to serve young people as they have always had—where the president who, after all, is the conscience of the institution, can work in a family-style Quaker-like democracy to achieve intellectual growth and educational progress.

There have been other changes too, and one of the most unfortunate is that in the case of too many presidents and other administrators, there is no longer a personal identification with an institution. It's more in the realm of a temporary take-care responsibility.

The role of coeducation has been a major one too. It has forced most all-male and to a lesser extent all-female institutions to take in the other sex. It has played havoc with the mechanical arrangements for dormitories. It has been synchronized with the burgeoning role of women. It is a far cry from the early days of Antioch, which was the first to take in women, but only in a lesser capacity relegating to them the household chores for the college.

The role of foundations, government or private, should not be forgotten. There has been so much money to be given out that the foundation executive has been forced into a role of playing God. In many cases foundations have been responsible for the creation of new empires within an institution, and because of outside funding, independent empires often bearing a tenuous allegiance to the institution and ready to shift loyalties when the least tampering with its independence is threatened. But often foundation grants petered out, and this created problems for the institution, for it meant usually that faculty salaries that had been paid by outside sources now had to be assumed by the college or university.

Computerization has also been a new factor in the last two decades, adding considerably to the general costs. In the case of larger universities, it has advanced considerably the speeding of experiments and research. It has become a respected, sophisticated, and necessary part of the instructional offerings, a far cry from the mathematical fare of generations ago.

It has been an age that spelled the gradual phasing out of the independent colleges as they were known at the turn of the century. Certainly very few new ones have been founded in the last few decades. Many have had to close their doors, some have been taken over by the states. With the exception of the relatively few astronomically-endowed, practically all are leading an uneasy existence.

There has been an overall homogenizing movement taking place. Private institutions become more and more state-related. Colleges that proclaimed the purity of their liberal arts offerings now talk excitedly of their career preparation. The converse is also true: curricula that were almost entirely professional such as engineering and business administration, are prodded to squeeze in more and more general cultural subjects.

Lastly, the proliferation of community colleges is changing the aspect of higher education. There will be a greater and greater proportion of college students who will be spending their formative years in such colleges, forcing four-year colleges into a new pattern—that of the last two years plus the masters, which really makes more sense.

It is with all this background of overall changes—all after World War II and mostly within the last two decades, that we must consider the role of the college or university president and other top-level administrators, for surely the ambiance has changed considerably.

Finally, it should be said that the day of great development is probably over. Institutions are already too large, and everybody recognizes this. Besides the money isn't there, and with the end of the baby boom, we shall probably not need any more college places. Presidents and other administrators will be kept so busy with other matters, unionization, computerization, communications, that they will have fewer creative impulses.

17

THE NEW PRESIDENT

WHAT SHOULD A NEW PRESIDENT DO DURING THE INITIAL get-acquainted period? First, he should read as much about the institution as he can. He probably will have done a great deal of this in his candidacy for the job. But now he has to dig deeper. He will look through the students publications, the clipping books, the articles in the various collegiate books of reference, the trustees' minutes. Other administrators and his secretary or the previous president's secretary, if his is new, can suggest important files to read through. It is an irksome job but a necessary one.

Second, he should look into every corner of the campus, making mental notes which he should transcribe later into written notes as soon as possible. He should not hesitate to peek into closets and washrooms. He should visit all buildings so that later he can embark on a strong maintenance program.

Third, he should get to know all the administrators, not only those in the instructional programs but in all the various sections of the institution: financial, publicity, custodial and legal. He should be briefed on the outstanding faculty members and know why they are important. This should be followed up by dropping into their classes to say hello or to invite them to come to his office.

In a small college he can meet individually most of the faculty. But depending on the size, he may have to break up the faculty into groups and organize special receptions, but with this admonition: no group should be so large that he can't study the names beforehand. A good plan is to supplement his previous study by having his secretary or the administrator in charge of the group present each member individually. It is well to invite the spouses because they too are part of the family.

Then he should arrange to meet with the student leaders in an informal atmosphere and ask them some questions about their feelings for the institution. He should be ready for three standard gripes: the food is terrible, some faculty members are poor teachers, tuition is too high.

The non-teaching staff should not be forgotten for they too have a part in the success or failure of an institution. It won't hurt an administrator to have people feel that he is human and interested in the auxiliary workers as well as the professors.

The least interesting of the studies he has to make is to find out how many committees there are and how they function. Generally, he will find that there are too many and that the amount of time and energy expended is far out of proportion to the contributions they make. Too many committees dehumanize the institution. Whether the incoming administrator can reduce this structure will depend on the particular situation. At any rate, it may be as difficult a task as trying to reduce the committees of Congress. From what I can observe, faculty are just as tired of lengthy, unproductive committee meetings as anyone else. Any possible curtailments may meet with relief by all parties concerned.

Then he has to tackle the problem of meeting community leaders and those who have been helping the institution. This will take a longer time and probably this process will develop even though he may not take the initiative.

If the institution serves mostly a circumscribed geographical area, it would not be amiss to invite the high school principals who send him the major number of his students. If his constituency comes from a much wider area or is national, I still think it might be well to invite key principals from a wider area. Perhaps he can do this by arranging an educational conference at the college. In other words, the new president has to make himself visible to as many constituencies as possible and in doing so, he will become that much more valuable to the institution.

There are still more aspects of the institution that the new president has to study. He should know all about the students' academic background: where they come from, the breakdown by sociological groups, financial background, future aspirations of students. One simple device is to have a large loose-leaf notebook with pages for each factual delineation. The director of admissions should prepare these sheets for him.

The new administrator has to know the union if one has been certified, and also about the other two unions that may be ever-ready to pounce upon the existing collective bargaining agent. Sometimes faculty members may belong to two of the three unions.

A study of the other colleges within the state is always in order. This is another fact sheet for the loose-leaf book. Usually, the state department of higher education can supply complete listings with addresses and phone numbers.

He has to get the feel of his alumni: what fields attract them, geographical distribution, leaders, age breakdown. Those, for instance in journalism can be especially useful. If he invites such a group to a luncheon or dinner meeting, usually they can be of enormous value to him in public relations, or if we want to put it more baldly, publicity. The alumni director can similarly arrange an informal dinner of the twenty or so major financial supporters among the alumni or the twenty best-known alumni (or alumnae). People are always impressed and feel honored in being invited by the president.

Along the way, he should arrange for a press conference and he should learn to do this often, especially if he has momentous news to announce. The various newspapers in his area will be glad to have an opportunity to size up the new president. It should be an informal meeting and tidbits about the family, about former position, about hobbies, about aspirations, are all grist for the mill.

Now for some specifics about his office and general routine. Even a new president of the United States upon taking office has to decide some of these seemingly minor matters. The new head must decide on his hours and schedule. He must decide on how to organize his office and especially his files. There are many letters that are not important enough to file, and yet one hesitates to throw away. I had a special double drawer where I would throw such letters or my replies. Every few months either I or my secretary would go through them quickly and pick out those few that had acquired some importance; the rest would be thrown away. I still use the same system. It saves filing space and it saves time. Another gimmick I had was to have a "trouble closet" with four rows of sixty-degree shelves for troublesome matters. I didn't want them lost in the file and I didn't want them staring me in the face. I would put them on the shelves. Whenever I felt like it, I would open the "trouble closet" and in a minute or two I could reassess the situation. Form letters should be regularized.

Each administrator has the right to have a few idiosyncracies. I abhor smoke, and as a matter of fact I am allergic to it. There was no reason why I should have had to suffer through someone else's polluting habits. I simply told my colleagues of my idiosyncracy and explained laughingly that unless it was a "$1,000 or more" donor, no smoking was the rule in my office. Another idiosyncracy I had was to have tomato juice with lemon juice added for all afternoon meetings. It was a welcome pick-me-up at the low point of the day. Or perhaps, one doesn't want anything but first class mail to enter the sacred portals. These matters seem small but they really aren't. It might be well to find out what has been causing tie-ups, grievances, rhubarbs or teeth-gnashing reaction around the presidential sphere of action and set up simple procedures that may avoid them. Lastly, the president has to decide on what community and professional societies he should join and this list is another sheet for the fact book.

This is a good time for a newly chosen president to reassess himself. What are the reasons an executive is chosen? He may look like the "executive" type. Or he may be an effective speaker. He may have come from a prestigious institution though on a lower executive level. Perhaps he is a renowned scholar or has published a great deal. He may have the requisite degrees and especially from prestige institutions. In some cases, the institution is hard up for candidates and has to fill the position. The executive chosen should ask himself "Why was I chosen?" and then seek to fill in lacunae.

But this is a good place to go over the litany of faults that an administrator can be accused of:

1. Laziness
2. Being physically or psychologically unfitted for the job
3. Being poorly informed
4. Having limited experience in education
5. Being a cultural cripple
6. Procrastination
7. Being disorganized
8. Being a publicity seeker, first, last and always
9. Spending his time on other activities rather than on the institution.
10. Having favorites
11. Being untrustworthy
12. Flying off the handle
13. Sitting too much in his office
14. Being unapproachable
15. Inventing too many reports and paper work
16. Making a poor appearance and not being able to speak in public
17. Playing his cards too close to the chest
18. Not being able to take criticism

It's a pretty devastating list. And yet none of these faults can really be ascertained to any great extent by the search committee. It's only when the new person is on the job that these faults begin to creep up. It's a good humbling check list for any administrator and perhaps he or she can do something to correct whatever flaws exist. Let him or her ask *mea culpa?*, and in all humility seek to overcome the failings that exist.

The necessity for protocol exists in any institution. Sometimes it may seem an unnecessary impediment. Why should one invite three boring associate professors when there is a sparkling assistant professor who would make a great guest. But our primary purpose is not to hurt peoples' feelings and to prevent jealousy and hatred. Depending on the size of the institution, it will be necessary, although at times it may seem artificial, to have meeting by rank, by campus, by departments, or whatever manageable group common sense would indicate. There has to be a sense of order apparent to all, and probably in most cases it will be for the best.

After making these various studies, the new administrator is in a position to establish priorities for his course of action. It's a comforting feeling when a person can say to himself: "I've done my homework; now this is what I'd like to move ahead on." At this point it might be well to have a conference with the chairman of the board to go over his plan of action. Perhaps the chairman might like to invite two or three key members to this conference. It won't hurt the new president to have the trustees know that he is tackling his job head on and it will be useful to him if they have suggestions for refining his priorities.

I would caution the new president however from rushing into false or artificial crash programs, realizing that all of these have some merit. But if a crash program upsets too drastically the even tenor of the institution's operation, if it is forced forward to the exclusion of other worthy elements, if it causes an unduly large expenditure, then it is time to be careful. There have been attempts to capture instant greatness by various devices. For instance, going after only the top ten percentile students and offering scholarships to them. Certainly, I say elsewhere that there must be an effort to attract meritòrious students but to "buy" a whole raft of top students is almost as bad as "buying" a whole coterie of athletes and may produce an unhealthy and resentful situation. Another ploy is to want to publicize the "highest faculty salaries in the country." With the exception of thirty or forty rich colleges which will have high but not excessively high salaries, except for special endowed chairs, most institutions can not afford this ploy. This ploy will prove to be short lived and will backfire. Sometimes an institution will try to bring in well-publicized faculty members, even though they teach little or not at all. Often the method will be to build super de luxe buildings or have dazzling publicity or try to have attention getting projects or to support unneeded doctoral programs. *Festina lente* is a good motto, especially if one doesn't have the money.

Having mapped the path for the new president, I would add that for other administrative offices, most of the items operate for them too. The one factor not involved is the relationship to the trustees since they would work through the president. A dean would be involved superficially with the entire campus, but chiefly in the areas under his supervision. A non-academic officer would not be involved with teaching matters, but most of the other items would be matters of interest. I would say that there is about eighty per cent overlapping of interests and about ninety five per cent if we realize that in committee work all of the points discussed will be involved at one time or another.

I believe that one of the weaknesses of institutions today is that there is a lack of communications in matters that are not strictly in one's bailiwick. One doesn't interfere, but when a matter comes up for general discussion, one should have an apperceptive background. Let me give two examples. An academic dean may not be concerned with food, but poor eating habits may be the cause of illness and this does impinge upon classroom attendance. A non-academic vice president may not be involved with admissions and yet the matter of parking spaces does depend on how many students drive to college or keep cars on the campus. Intelligent overview does make for better administration.

18

PRESSURES ON PRESIDENTS

WE MUST SEEK TO fiND A BALANCE FOR PSYCHOLOGICAL AND physiological racing, to measure out our competition for increasing achievement and leadership. We must seek to find a midpoint between self destructive stress and an unimaginative, lifeless pattern of working.

We operate as college administrators much the same way as any executive does, whether in politics, in a bureaucracy, or in a business or industry. First of all, nothing means anything in life unless we have a conscience and this requires constant resharpening and adjusting to avoid the smugness and the rationalizing of uncouth acts. Further, we must have a genuine love for what we are doing, for the institution we are serving, for the clientele we are seeking to help, for our fellow workers in spite of the faults we may see in them. We must enjoy a sense of creating, a freedom albeit very restricted at times, to forge new paths. The role of leadership involves a feeling of mastery, a sense of confidence in oneself. All of these factors are subject to forces outside of ourselves, to what Machiavelli calls "fortuna," to the chances of fate, to movements over which we have no control. Lastly, a healthy economic state can help us to overcome many of the unfortunate turns that develop from day to day or year to year.

An administrator takes pleasure in having people look up to him and this includes members of his own family. Generally, this will also be true of his fellow workers, although if they sense weakness in him they will question his sense of fitness. Jealousy also plays a part in their reactions. It is for that reason that the administrator must first of all have the personal and professional maturity required for his position.

Let's ask the question: "Why does a person want to become a top administrator?"

1. To make more money
2. The position represents a distinct honor and a distinct step ahead
3. It may be a stepping stone to a higher honor outside of education
4. For the president of a smaller institution it may be a stepping stone to the presidency of a more important institution.
5. The office is forced upon him and it may be a case of noblesse oblige.
6. There may exist a desire to serve one's alma mater or there is a feeling of devotion in serving the cause of the city, or the state.
7. The person may have a genuine desire to work out an educational breakthrough.
8. He may seek a sinecure until retirement
9. The person may have a basic urge for power

If the answer to one or more of these questions is in the affirmative then he has to be ready to pay the price.

If he has no real desire to serve then he should give up the post. Assuming that he is impelled by affirmative motives, then he has to think clearly on the ordered but turbulent life of an administrator.

It may be of interest to review two surveys that I had made on behalf of the International Association of University Presidents, of which I was president, and by the American Institute of Management, on pressures that discourage college presidents. In the first survey, made in 1965, the greatest single factor was the skyrocketing costs. In the second round, this factor had descended to the fourth place, probably because of three factors as far as we could analyze: one, the major thrust of building had taken place; two, institutions were used to high costs where they occurred; and three, where high costs were due to faculty or nonfaculty salaries, a leveling-off process was taking place.

The inability to make the institution as outstanding as the president would like to make it stood almost as high in the first survey and number one in the second. Curiously, this was a pressure not only in a small, relatively unknown college but also in large and prestigious institutions.

The pressures of a rat race schedule was a strong third in the original survey and strong runner-up in the second survey five years later. I can understand this and a follow-up analysis pointed out what contributed to the rat race: committee meetings, trustees' meetings and conferences, administrative councils, faculty confrontations, student interviews, community affairs and service clubs, speeches, filing of reports, budgetary approvals, fund-raising appointments, appointments with friends asking for special favors, professional associations, meetings, town and gown problems, newspaper interviews, necessary social functions, an avalanche of reports to be read, alumni gripe sessions and just plain everyday memoranda and correspondence. At the end of the day, the president feels that, in spite of the succession of events, all he has done is to go through motions that don't lead anywhere. The sheer drudgery is devastating. The monotony of each succeeding day presenting more of the same trivia is a depressing experience. There is no feeling of progress or of the élan of creative activity, merely a deadening routine that is not much different than that of a complaint clerk in a large department store. And yet, probably something does come out of it all, even though it may be depressing to go through meaningless and time-wasting meetings, or the ritualistic back slapping, whether it be with alumni, community representatives or university colleagues. Most of these pressures apply to the other administrative positions.

I personally have found that I accomplished my most creative work on Sundays and holidays during my summer stays in Maine. This was the work that gave me the greatest sense of accomplishment. It was in Maine that I mapped out the development of both the Teaneck and Florham-Madison campuses, of our Wroxton College in England, and of Edward Williams College in Hackensack, New Jersey. I received my mail daily and I replied immediately either by telephone or by dictaphone. Any of my administrators could telephone me at will to get quick decisions. I would fly back from time to time to oversee things, to attend important meetings, or in emergencies. But I was not interrupted by trivia. By late morning, I was ready to think about the important overall developments of the university. When a problem is at hand, the best way is to lock oneself in where people can not get to one or perhaps tackle it in the morning from seven to nine or during a weekend. It is best to try to do it straight through. If one tries to do it a little at a time, one has to pick up pieces and waste time getting back on the track. It is inefficient to work in dribs and drabs.

The next two pressures are the unreasonable demands of professors and of students. Both demands have been escalating during the last few years and will probably continue to do so, the former especially because of the trend toward professional unionization. Here again, the administrator has to have time to reflect objectively on what is right for the overall development of the institution and what is just for the ultimate service it proposes to give to students. After receiving various points of view from faculty, from other administrators, from outside sources, from students, and once a consensus has been reached, then he has to have the courage to take his stand in a forth-right manner in spite of the brickbats that are sure to come. The important thing for the administrator is that this stance has been arrived at in a thorough and objective manner and that his conscience is clear. An administrator can not run a popularity contest nor can he administer an institution on the basis of flitting love pats. I always looked for four things in an administrator.

1. Does he have a conscience?
2. Does he work hard at his task?
3. Does he have professional expertise?
4. Does he have a modest amount of imagination?

All of which leads to another great pressure that causes many heartaches for presidents—the inefficiency of administrators. As one president described it, "I find myself coming in at eight in the morning, working through the day until ten or eleven in the evening. In the meantime, my administrators breeze in at ten or so, enjoy long and leisurely lunch hours, and are on their way home in midafternoon 'to beat the traffic.' They lose no opportunity to attend professional meetings, while I stay at my work minding the store for them. In the meantime, I'm waiting for reports and decisions that never arrive because everyone is at time-wasting pipe-smoking sessions." *male / angway*

One would immediately ask "Well, why not get rid of inefficient administrators?" It isn't that easy. First of all, in academic circles there is a great sense of human compassion and a tendency not to be abrasive and run roughshod over lesser administrators. Then again, in most cases, an administrator returns to his tenured position of professor so that in breaking an administrator, the president winds up with a dedicated enemy. Lastly, it is becoming more and more usual for chairmen, deans, and other officers to be selected by faculty committees, and under such circumstances it becomes almost impossible or at least inadvisable for the president to terminate abruptly such a selection. What is happening more often is that such a faculty-elected officr is discontinued by his very electors because he is not catering to their demands of interests consistently enough. This doesn't make sense administratively. An administrative officer can not be a shop steward.

Inability to get rid of unworthy faculty members also seemed to be one of the great frustrations of administrators and with increasing unionism this source of administrative unhappiness is bound to become greater.

While the origin of the tenure system goes back some years, as we have seen, and was intended to prevent summary dismissal of those whose religious views were at variance with official church doctrines, now it covers just about everything and the tendency of faculty review committees is to be overprotective towards faculty members whose contracts are not recommended for renewal.

Impending financial disaster worries perhaps thirty five per cent of the private college presidents and this is understandable. Every year, twenty or thirty colleges close their doors, most of them private institutions. The proliferation of tax-supported institutions is beginning to take its toll.

The inflationary spiral, mainly in faculty salaries and also in building and maintenance costs of structures necessitated by "trying to keep up with the Joneses," has increased far more than tuition increases, which in turn have a deceptive character. A faculty member may glibly figure that increasing tuition, let us say $300, and multiplying that $300 by the number of students will give X dollars which divided by Y number of faculty members will come to Z dollars for each. But a knowledgeable president or administrative officer will realize four things, most of which are operative in almost all cases:

1. The increase will be needed to match retroactive expenses
2. Probably one third to fifty percent should go for additional student grants or scholarships
3. The increase in tuition is partially intended to offset overall inflationary expenses in all areas, not only in faculty salaries. To give a few examples: social security, advertising, food costs, general supplies and book prices.
4. Every faculty increase involves sympathetic upward movements for all other categories: administrative, office staff, custodial and cafeteria employees. Faculty groups and now legal faculty bargaining agents are decidedly self-

centered in the matter of faculty salaries, and understandably so. There is no use getting angry about it; one has to realize it is a fact of life. The president and the board of trustees have to rise above all this and think in terms of the entire college or university family.

Other pressures included:

1. inability to get really outstanding students
2. ragging by the student newspapers
3. inability to control things

Let's look at the problem from another angle. What are the elements that lead to what Professor Harry Levinson of Harvard calls "executive malaise" and let us remember that this can happen in politics, in business, or in education. The first is fear of failure. The second is the impingement of one's professional pressures on family or personal life. The third is the utter dependency on specialists so that the administrator feels he is just a clerk carrying out someone's dictates. Who are these specialists who may keep a president in subjection? The computer expert, the fund-raising consultant, the state bureaucrat who oversees higher education, the union delegate who is ready to extend his domain, to name a few. Fifty years ago these people were nonexistent or practically so. Now they are all on hand ready to give the college president a sense of inferiority and to proclaim the importance of their position and to insist that he (the president) give up his prerogatives in the special sphere. His loneliness is another factor—the feeling that he can not get too close to his subordinates.

The feeling of physical deterioration tends to undermine the executive; the lack of physical energy tends to accumulate quickly to demoralize the person; the feeling that no one appreciates what he is doing, whether the trustees, the faculty, his fellow administrators, the students, or the community, can and does crush the spirit. Finally, the feeling that what one is doing is not important and isn't leading anywhere can be a crushing blow.

Of all the destructive elements that cause stress, anger and hate are the worst. The administrator functions best in an atmosphere of mutual trust and respect, with equanimity and with serenity. Frustration may lead to anger; continual opposition to hate. It was no glib assertion when Woodrow Wilson on assuming the Presidency said, "after Princeton, Washington is pie." And yet anger and hate are apt to be a part of any administrative position and have to be avoided and contained.

It sounds terrible, but it need not be so. The first thing is to keep one's self physically and nutritionally on a high level. Second, colleges are overloaded with statistics and it might be well to diminish them to those that are necessary and usable. The administrator must acquire the feeling that what he is doing has a worthwhile social function. He has to be sincere and candid with his faculty, and while he has to be willing to listen at all times, he must assume leadership. He has to know how to build on strengths and these may be found anywhere—not only in his faculty but in students, in trustees, in alumni, in community leaders. He has to know how to encourage self development by his fellow workers and how to stimulate teamwork. Lastly, he has to have genuine love for his colleagues and an intense desire to serve the students. It is this love, above everything else, that will give balance and serenity to his life.

19

WARDING OFF RETROGRESSION

WHAT WE MUST GUARD AGAINST IN COLLEGES AND UNIVER-
sities is to proceed on the assumption that the more
money we spend, the better service we give to the students. This is a problem that affects all segments of
government, whether it be on the federal, state, or city
level. We have all seen how bureaucracy expands without benefitting the taxpayer or consumer and in fact
giving him less for more money. In education we have
been dazzled by grandiose buildings and we make easy
assumptions that bigger is better. In the meantime, in
the very midst of burgeoning costs, the seeds of deterioration are sown. Most private colleges, unless they have
vigorous and knowledgeable leadership, are particularly prone to retrogression, especially when the competition is rough and the available money is minimal.

What happens when a college begins to retrogress?
The most devastating development is that everybody,
faculty, administrators, office personnel, other non-
academic personnel, begins to cut out a little piece of

territory and makes it as worthwhile and as convenient for himself or herself as possible. In the absence of strong administrative direction and supervision, everyone arranges things to suit himself and naturally everyone likes it that way. Each person rationalizes that it doesn't make too much difference in the total complex. And as one person spreads out or assigns to himself some special privilege or physical advantage, the others are sure to copy. Courage to waste, to duplicate, to expand, to take life easier, is easily assimilated. The sum total is devastating for the institution and in the end, the cost of wastage is borne either by the student or by the taxpayer or in some cases by donors and in a few cases by all three.

The second thing that happens is that admission standards go down, almost imperceptibly each year. It is true that we put too much emphasis at times on standardized tests and high school grades and don't look below for true and unused potential. And it is equally true that these days all academic standards are lowered because of political and civil rights pressures, and most important because the validity of basic college entrance tests is being questioned. But the academic community does have to operate within a framework of standards. I don't know of any institution that has made a reputation for itself by being nonselective except one— Parsons—and it was demolished by the accreditation association for doing so.

In the deteriorating institution, the process of digging deeper into the barrel takes place over a period of years. The public statements are always hypocritically to the contrary. But the real place to get the true story is in the high school guidance offices. After all, they know how easily students can get into certain colleges. If you look at the history of colleges in America you will find that sixty or seventy years ago, certain colleges were in the ascendancy. If you look at the picture today, many of these colleges are relatively unknown.

The third thing that happens is that physically the campus begins to take on a worn look. The ivy covers up some of the deterioration, of course. The furniture, whether in the classrooms or in the offices, becomes ill-assorted. Very little new building takes place, if at all. Thus while other institutions burst forth in resplendent new buildings, the obsolescent ones sink further back into a decaying atmosphere.

Fourth, there is a lack of educational élan. To be sure there will be all kinds of sanctimonious reports and statements by administrators and faculty committees on what they propose to do. There will be nebulous references to old traditions, to the importance of teaching students to think, to the necessity for keeping entrenched courses as they are. In the meantime, everyone makes sure nothing is done to disturb the status quo. Here and there there may be a flicker sparked by a modest foundation grant. The flicker goes out simultaneously with the end of the grant. A new president may come in; he may dance around the fringe of the college for a few years. After a while, either he settles back into a comfortable posture hoping that things will last until he is ready for retirement, or he goes elsewhere.

Lastly there is an all-pervasive anonymity that engulfs the institution. An institution can not stand still. Either it must move forward or it sinks into oblivion. There are almost 3,000 colleges and universities in America. How many of them does one know or read about? And, as an institution sinks back into that sea of anonymity, it becomes more and more difficult for it to come out of the doldrums. The process may be described as the slow death of an educational institution.

But the greatest deterioration is caused by wastage. It may be that a college has more space than is needed, and that naturally the upkeep of the unneeded space is an expense that can not be avoided. This probably happens more often in public institutions, not because administrators of such institutions are more wasteful than others, but simply because so many new public colleges have been created without knowing what the real needs were going to be, and before the permanent staff was on the job. At other times, it may be due to the fact that a lump sum is arbitrarily decided on for the capital expenses and once the pattern has been set, the spending process moves ahead inexorably. Or it may be because of a desire for architectural splendor unmatched by other institutions. This is a form of political conspicuous spending. Rich private institutions usually have a well padded endowment that can soften the impact of wastage or conspicuous consumption if you will.

Some of this is repetitive, but since finances are so important in the reaching of educational goals, it bears restating in slightly different form. Let us keep in mind that in a private college we have to keep two things in balance—remuneration to the faculty and tuition charged to students. Too many private colleges have been led astray by the decisions of the few very rich colleges, which represent perhaps two percent of the total number. Out of 2,000 or so private institutions, about 40 may be very rich. First of all, they have become in the last three decades very selective. If such a college takes students in the top five per cent, increasing tuition doesn't decrease their numbers. At most, they might have to lower their standards and take them from the top ten per cent, which is still very selective—far more selective than in most private colleges. About 200 to 300 private colleges are somewhat selective, taking students from the upper half; the remainder are nonselective. Increasing tuition in the case of all but the very rich produces two dangers: loss of students or a dangerous lowering of standards.

But take the case of the Ivy League institutions. They will tend to have more applications from wealthy families. Increasing the tuition for a family in the $50,000 to $100,000 a year income does not produce too much of a problem. And a family, let us say, in the $15,000 a year class will gladly take out a second mortgage on the home so that a son or daughter can go to Harvard, Princeton or Yale. But it doesn't quite happen that way. Most of these applicants have such good test scores that they come in with their own scholarships from high school, state, or federal funds. For those not covered and in need of financial help, the rich colleges have a sackful of special endowment scholarships to draw upon or even upon general endowment funds. After all, if a university has $20,000 endowment income per student to spend, an extra thousand or two to go on scholarships doesn't pose much of a problem. Most private colleges don't have this advantage.

If a private college doesn't want to lose students, doesn't want to lower standards and still wants to be competitive in faculty salaries, the only way to do it is to avoid waste. Until the last war, most colleges operated with parsimonious economy. During the war they were kept alive through service programs. After the war, when veterans began to come back, all institutions went through what was probably the most chaotic period in higher education—the era of the veteran rush. There was a readjustment in the early fifties, fatal to many college presidencies unprepared for the sudden drop in enrollment. But soon there was a healthy revival when everybody wanted to go to college, and by the early

sixties the war babies had grown to college age. The
states were pumping money into public institutions and
these were beginning to take over more and more the
services provided by private institutions.

State higher education planning bodies will almost
always plan for public institutions to take care of every
student within the state who wants to go to college.
There is a distinct disinclination to allow for the role of
the private college, which heretofor had been taking
care of a large percentage of the state's need, often more
than half. Part of this stems from the antipathy to
church-related colleges, forgetting that it was the
churches that started higher education in America.
Sometimes the reason given is that most of the students
in private colleges come from out-of-state and that the
public institutions are serving the in-state students.
This isn't quite true. In each state, private institutions
take care of a very appreciable part of the instate students. No matter how many facilities a state builds, an
appreciable number of students within that state will
want to go out of state anyway. This was very forcibly
brought out by Dr. Eckles in his New York State report
of 1966. Dr. Eckles stated that students like to get away
from home—usually at least 150 miles. Let us take the
situation in the East: New York, Pennsylvania, Ohio,
and Massachusetts have the greatest number of private
institutions and send to each other the greatest number
of students. These four states are also among those doing the most for public colleges. If each of these four
states builds facilities to take care of all the in-state students, one can well imagine the problem this creates for
the many private colleges within those four states
alone.

The result of all this is that by the eighties, there are
so many places in public colleges that enrollment in

private colleges has begun to shrink very seriously. The private colleges have made the situation worse by pricing themselves out of the market. In the meantime, during a period of bursting enrollments and easy money, all colleges have fallen into wasteful habits, the most sinful of which is that very human inclination towards empire building—both in old areas of administration and in new fringe activities. Every time someone dreams up a new tangential area of service, a director has to be chosen to supervise the activity. The director then clamors for an assistant. Both have to have secretaries and the first requisition is for an expensive duplicating machine for the avalanche of reports and memoranda that will issue forth. Often the pump is primed by a foundation grant, but by the time the grant is discontinued the new office is heavily entrenched. It might be well for trustees and the president to have a large wall chart showing all such projects, the number of employees involved, with their salaries, and the total expenditures, including travel and expense accounts.

The business of a college is to focus on the development of young people. Rich universities, whether private or public, like rich nations, can afford the luxury of wasting money. Most private colleges dependent on undergraduate tuition have no right to dissipate their meager resources on questionable sideshows.

Another area of crippling expenses is in the area of low enrollment courses. It would be well to have, each semester, a list of all courses with enrollment of less than twelve. Sometimes a college has a moral obligation to give a certain course even though it may have low enrollment, simply because that course has been promised in the fulfillment of a major. Often things slip by for a number of reasons, most because of administrative carelessness. It doesn't make sense to have three low-enrollment classes in a certain subject when two normal classes would do. Or worse still, to have a tail-end class of six that could easily be split up and added to the other two classes, whether normal or low. Sometimes, a low-enrollment subject can be given every other year. Or, if the college has an evening session, it can be given in the evening in order to pick up a few extra evening students who want the course but could not attend it during the day. Some strange things happen in colleges. I know of a poet-in-residence who was bragging of how few hours he had to teach. He had been appointed to teach four undergraduate courses. Each one had five or six students in it. He then proceeded to combine his classes so that he wound up with two classes. On an hourly basis, he was the most expensive teacher in the school, even though he was a young fellow of less than national reputation.

I knew of another person, an art teacher, who was appointed similarly as a full-time instructor with four classes to teach, which he did for the first year. But by the second year, because of changing and slipshod administrative attention, he had managed to put his four classes all on one day and evening, spending the rest of his time in his studio in the city, and incidentally with his mistress. It was a blurred sort of studio activity—students coming in *à volonté* if at all. Eighty percent of this man's activity was not in the college—it was elsewhere. The college was paying full salary for a part-time faculty member. It was really subsidizing the artist, which is commendable if you have the money. Considering the college's meager resources, it would have made much more sense for it to have invited him to spend one day a week at the college and to pay him on a part-time basis. The art majors were getting an inade-

quate approach to art by a man who was not particularly a leader in his field. It would have made much
more sense to change the category to visiting artist and
have a different point of view each year. Or, perhaps
instead of having one full salary allocated to one man,
to invite two or three artists as adjunct part-time
teachers, as they do at the Art Students League in New
York.

There are probably hundreds of small private colleges
in the country living on the edge of bankruptcy, where
some faculty members are pulling more than their
weight to balance the minuscule classes of other colleagues, or where undergraduates are paying for the
imbalance created by small classes. Common sense
should be a good guide in all of this. One doesn't need a
computer or a foundation grant to solve these relatively
simple problems. In an institution where, because of
conditions beyond its control, there exists a precarious
financial situation, inequities should be shared equally
by all members of the faculty.

A third area of wastage is in the physical administration of the campus. Admittedly, an academic administrator is rarely qualified as a business manager and
tends to leave everything to the non-academic direction
of campus facilities. And yet it isn't as simple as all that.
This is an area where the consultative expertise of the
trustees can be drawn upon—not to direct or give orders, but to study and suggest. Every dollar wasted
here has to be drawn from academic services or
reflected in higher tuition. Empire building will take
place here as it does in the academic sphere. But the
opportunities for wastage are even more rampant, ranging all the way from excessive use of paper to the quiet
laying aside of old model machines, hearkening to the

blandishments of glib salesmen touting the latest model, from the hoarding of unneeded secretaries to the creation of comfortable niches for esoteric services.

Efficiency studies, unpalatable as they may be to those ensconced in easy schedules, are very much in order. Why should it be necessary to have a three hundred per cent rise in administrative costs when the number of students remained the same in one private institution of which I knew? Who checks on the heating oil received, or is the delivery hose directed back into the tank truck, as happened in an actual case? The same human motives operate in academic circles as in any other sphere of activity, and in any institution where hundreds of thousands of dollars are involved in goods and services, the temptations for a dishonest dollar are always persistent. In an institution of 600, inefficiency or downright dishonesty can easily add $300 to the undergraduate's bill. In an academic institution, it is easy to get into a habit of easy, permissive ways. There has to be an air of parsimonious economy! Just because needless items may have insinuated themselves into the budget, that doesn't mean the money has to be expended. There should be checks on budget expenditures every three months or so. There needs to be an immediate check on those overspending, and curiously, a peeking into the areas where the expenditures are not being made. Why were the allocations made initially?

Lastly, the board of trustees has to decide on the extent of athletics and physical training. It is my belief, and I may be in a minority, that we have allowed the expenses in this area to run away with themselves in many institutions. I believe strongly in lifetime sport activities which can cost relatively little. The lesser emphasis should be on spectator sports. Super de luxe sport structures cost a lot of money, in amortizing, in maintenance, in faculty personnel, and the undergraduate is paying for it. I have analyzed a number of small college budgets and it may be surprising to find out that it may cost the undergraduate $500 or more out of his tuition for the country club privileges he may be enjoying. I regret that with all this expenditure we still are missing the boat on some important aspects of physical development, such as nutrition, corrective exercise, and self-defense, as well as leisure time sport activities that include socializing aspects, such as fishing, dancing and mountain walking. In other words, too often we are involved in a wasteful, imbalanced, educationally unjustifiable program that is helping to push private colleges into a financial abyss.

20

EPILOGUE

A GREAT MANY THINGS HAVE BEEN LEFT OUT OF THIS BOOK. I did not try to take up everything, as one would in a formal textbook. Each one of us in the administrative field emphasizes certain things and as our institutions develop the configuration changes from year to year. It changes for a number of reasons. First, as an institution expands, the pressure forces us to delegate certain matters whether we like it or not. Second, assistants will vary in their capabilities and interests. The result is that we will concentrate on those areas that develop the greatest weaknesses. Third, our own interest change from year to year. One year we may become excited about a new building. When we have had our fill of building problems, we may want to forget about construction and concern ourselves with something else. Fourth, emergencies arise from year to year. It may be a fund-raising drive; it may be a sudden unforseen drop in enrollment. Fifth, the college president may be directed by his board of trustees to concentrate on a certain phase of the work.

One college president stated that perhaps we need to see our problems as a whole in order that they may appear attractive to us. When we deal with them separately, they are just plain jobs. We do see problems as a whole, but we do this best when we are away from the pressing items of the moment, when we are relaxed, when our minds are not cluttered with annoying and irritating details. I would also add that the broad decisions are the easiest and the most pleasurable to make. Usually we have been mulling them over for a long time and then suddenly the opportunity arises for a decision. It may seem that the decision has been made almost on the spur of the moment, but it really hasn't. It has been a long time usually in the making.

I might have spoken about administrative patterns, but that would have been a waste of words because one might almost say that there are as many administrative patterns as there are small colleges. It really boils down to the men and women who are serving the college. If all is working well, they will divide the problems among themselves under the leadership of the president. Once the pattern is set, everyone has to know how he or she fits into the general order of things.

I probably should have said more about community relations. Here again the diversity is so great that it is almost staggering to attempt to point out all the various forms. Certainly it would be trite to say that a college has an obligation to foster the closest and the most harmonious community relations possible. Some institutions are coeducational community colleges, and others are exclusively women's boarding institutions. Some are completely religious in character, others are nonsectarian. Some are very limited in their curricular offerings, others may be able to offer a wide variety of courses to the community. In each case, the extent of possible cooperation with the community necessarily changes. And yet some broad statements can be made. A college, no matter what its own make-up, has a moral responsibility to have the people in its community in some way participate in the offerings and activities of the college. Now that many women are desirous of training for a middle-age career or wish to study for credits toward a degree, the opportunities are boundless for a college. Retired men and women often want to take courses to widen their horizons and this is another service a college should offer. These challenges to the faculty are good, not only financially but as a counterbalance to the sameness of teaching young college students. In many cases, young and old can be put in the same classroom with inspiration to both groups. The college community is changing and it's all to the good.

The problem of tax exemption is bound to be a sensitive one in most tax-conscious communities. The president has to be ready at all times to cope with it and to justify if necessary the tax exemption for a new acquisition of land or house. Then there is the matter of esthetic appearance. A college should add to the appearance of the area, and I don't believe we can take it for granted that this always is so. Colleges can become run down and slipshod in their "front lawn habits" just as industrial concerns or inconsiderate neighbours sometimes do. A college also has some obligation to see to it that the students observe reasonable standards of dress and deportment. In the Middle Ages, university students killed, fought, stole, and raped with impunity. We read with horror of the insolent attitude of the students of yore. But there are too many cases today where students feel they can be as discourteous, as unruly, as sloppy, as inconsiderate as they care to be. Hopefully it is a passing phase and undoubtedly somewhere along the line, someone is gaining a few dollars in the process, but it still is a phase that the college has to watch.

Every so often, a college president has to measure his progress. There are five important factors that can measure a president's success in his job. And these can be applied at the end of each five-year period:

1. Have I made the college give better service to the student?
2. Is my faculty a better one than it was five years ago?
3. Does the college have a better reputation than it had five years ago?
4. Is it better known?
5. Is the plant better?

It won't be easy to make this evaluation. But, it will be a reminder to have a sort of flywheel evenness to your college and it may spur concentrating on overcoming weaknesses.

I believe I can best sum up what a college should stand for when I state that it is a gathering of teachers, non-teaching workers, and students where all are active to provide the greatest possible opportunities for all to mature, and where everyone is striving to be as friendly and as considerate as possible to his fellow worker. It is as simple as that. But if there isn't an underlying feeling of idealism, of service and of companionship, then everything else is of no avail. But I hasten to add that in order to provide the best opportunity for these goals to be realized, it is important to pay attention to the mechanics of everyday operation. A college president must almost be all things to all persons. His life will find the greatest meaning in the spirit of service; it will find the greatest peace of mind through an orderly resolution of everyday operation.